PROJECT AIR FORCE

T0302773

Air Force Institutional Requirements

Opportunities for Improving the Efficiency of Sourcing, Managing, and Manning Corporate Requirements

Lisa M. Harrington, Kathleen Reedy, Paul Emslie, Darrell D. Jones, Tara L. Terry

Prepared for the United States Air Force

For more information on this publication, visit www.rand.org/t/RR1596

Library of Congress Cataloging-in-Publication Data is available for this publication.
ISBN: 978-0-8330-9593-0

Published by the RAND Corporation, Santa Monica, Calif.
© Copyright 2017 RAND Corporation
RAND® is a registered trademark.

Support RAND
Make a tax-deductible charitable contribution at
www.rand.org/giving/contribute

www.rand.org

Preface

In recent years, the Air Force has found it increasingly difficult to fill manpower authorizations in many career fields—not only operational and staff positions that support mission demands but also additional requirements that are levied on career fields. One source of these additional requirements is *institutional requirements*. Institutional requirements are valid, funded manpower requirements that do not align with a traditional, functional career field but are needed to support the Air Force institution—positions such as recruiters, instructors, generalist staff officers, or operational support.

The challenge for career field managers is that institutional requirements compete with operational requirements for the same pool of personnel. These assignments may also have an effect on the career development of individual officers. In some cases, the experience provided by an institutional requirement assignment is considered positive and contributes to an officer's competitiveness for future assignments and promotions. Other positions are considered a side-track, preventing officers from acquiring the depth of experience in their operational specialty that they would otherwise. Some career field managers, such as those in space and cyber, believe the impact of institutional requirements on manning and career development is serious enough to warrant formal study.

Thus, Air Force leadership in the offices of the Deputy Chief of Staff, Operations (AF/A3), and the Deputy Chief of Staff, Manpower, Personnel and Services (AF/A1), asked RAND Project AIR FORCE to examine the Air Force's institutional requirements and help determine whether there is a better way to source, manage, and man these service needs in the future. The Air Force also asked RAND to develop a method to assess the impact of manning institutional requirements on the ability of officer career fields to fill their core positions and apply this methodology to the space career field.

This report presents an assessment of the processes and policies for manning institutional requirements, addressing some of the unique challenges that arise in filling positions in particular categories of institutional requirements and offering recommendations to help the Air Force improve manning for institutional requirements while preserving the health of career fields. A companion report, *Using RAND's Military Career Model to Evaluate the Impact of Institutional Requirements on the Air Force Space Officer Career Field* (Rothenberg et al., 2017) describes a methodology to assess the impact of institutional requirements on a particular career field.

The research reported here was commissioned by the U.S. Air Force and conducted within the Manpower, Personnel, and Training Program of RAND Project AIR FORCE as part of a fiscal year 2015 project, "Institutional Requirements: Impact on Manning Across the Air Force."

RAND Project AIR FORCE

RAND Project AIR FORCE (PAF), a division of the RAND Corporation, is the U.S. Air Force's federally funded research and development center for studies and analyses. PAF provides the Air Force with independent analyses of policy alternatives affecting the development, employment, combat readiness, and support of current and future air, space, and cyber forces. Research is conducted in four programs: Force Modernization and Employment; Manpower, Personnel, and Training; Resource Management; and Strategy and Doctrine. The research reported here was prepared under contract FA7014-06-C-0001.

Additional information about PAF is available on our website: www.rand.org/paf/.

This report documents work originally shared with the U.S. Air Force on July 30, 2015. The draft report, issued on October 27, 2015, was scrutinized by U.S. Air Force subject-matter experts and formal peer reviewers.

Contents

Figures and Tables

Figures

Tables

Summary

In an era of force reductions and shrinking military budgets, core U.S. Air Force career field managers and personnel continue to feel the effects of prolonged undermanning. Most career field managers are unable to fully man their associated authorizations and are acutely aware of additional requirements that further reduce their available manpower pool. One significant source of these additional requirements is *institutional requirements* (IRs). IRs are valid, funded manpower requirements that do not align with a traditional, functional career field but are needed to support the Air Force institution—positions such as recruiters, instructors at accession sources, and generalist staff officers. In general, officers from any career field can fill an IR position, though there are exceptions for some IR positions with unique educational or experiential requirements.

Because they lack a formal career field manager and are often seen as a lower priority than operational career fields, IRs will be increasingly difficult to fill if the manpower system becomes less disciplined and competition for manpower intensifies. Space and cyber career field managers believe that the impact of IRs on their ability to man their core authorizations is serious enough to warrant formal study. Thus, Air Force leadership in the offices of the Deputy Chief of Staff, Operations (AF/A3) and the Deputy Chief of Staff, Manpower, Personnel and Services (AF/A1) asked RAND Project AIR FORCE to examine the Air Force's institutional requirements and help determine whether there is a better way to source, manage, and man these service needs in the future.

This report presents our assessment of the IR system, addressing some of the unique challenges that arise in filling positions in particular categories of IRs, and offers recommendations and alternative models for how to staff these corporate requirements. In developing these recommendations, we examined and drew on approaches used by the other military services and in the private sector to meet similar corporate needs.

The data for these assessments and recommendations come from a variety of sources. Very little information on the IR process at any level is officially documented, so the descriptions of the current status of IRs and the challenges in filling these positions largely derive from discussions with key stakeholders, including officials at the Air Force Personnel Center (AFPC), numerous IR-using organizations, career field managers and other Air Force personnel officials at various levels, and the equivalents of these officials in the other services. We obtained data on current and historical IR authorizations and manning from AFPC. Assessments from industry are from secondary-source literature and consultations with experts in the field.

The Process

Seventeen Air Force specialties are designated as IRs. In our analysis, we excluded a few specialties (competitive, high-profile assignments that are always filled) and combined the remaining specialties into several categories based on shared traits. Only positions from O-1 to O-5 in these specialties are counted as IRs; O-6 requirements and assignments are managed by a completely separate organization and subject to a different process. Our analysis included positions filled by nonrated officers because rated officers fill a disproportionately small number of positions and are assigned through a completely different process. We focused on the following categories of IRs (specialty codes in parentheses):

- strategy (16FX, 16PX)
- operations staff (16GX, 16RX)
- accession source command (80C0, 81C0)
- academic instruction and management (81T0, 82A0)
- recruiting (83R0)
- operations command and control (C2) and management (86M0, 86P0)
- inspections (87XX)
- senior leader support (88A0, 97E0).

These categories comprised a total of 2,813 positions at the end of fiscal year (FY) 2014, one-third of which were academic instruction and management. Of these 2,813 positions, only 2,007 were filled in FY 2014, though fill rates varied considerably by category. Senior leader support and recruiters had the highest manning percentages (above 100 percent in FY 2014); operations C2 and management, along with inspections, had the lowest, at only 55 percent.

An important characteristic of IRs is the lack of strategic oversight that determines and prioritizes functional community requirements in a traditional career field structure. Because there is no traditional career field structure, IR positions must be filled through alternative means—namely, through a *tax and draft* process. During three assignment cycles (spring, summer, and fall), functional career fields are called upon to assign a certain number of officers to fill these positions. Career field assignment teams are often reluctant to give up their personnel, especially if they are unable to fill all the positions within their career field. At the same time, organizations that own these positions, which we refer to as *IR-using organizations*, require these officers and may struggle to perform their missions when these positions go unfilled.

There is a perception among career field managers that the "burden" of filling IRs has increased in recent years, especially with cuts to Air Force end strength, and that filling these positions limits their ability to fill their own required positions by an even greater degree than in the past. This tug of war between IR-using organizations and functional career fields, and the likelihood that it will persist, motivates the need to identify new approaches to meeting these important Air Force requirements.

Reducing the Impact of Institutional Requirements

There are many opportunities to improve the IR process that can lessen the impact on career fields that must fill these requirements. These potential reforms can benefit both the using organizations and the career fields that must supply individuals to fill the positions. In general, most of the reforms identified here have some application to all categories of IRs, but new strategies for filling these positions must be tailored specifically to each IR category based on its unique characteristics, as we discuss in detail in Chapter Four. We identified promising solutions in six areas.

Address Overall Air Force Undermanning

A major challenge common to all IRs is systematic, long-term undermanning of funded authorizations. Until many of these Air Force–wide manning issues are addressed, challenges associated with filling IR positions cannot be fully resolved. Indeed, if the overall numbers of available officers and authorized positions were more in balance, many of the concerns associated with filling institutional requirements—from the perspective of both the career fields and IR-using organizations—would diminish. Despite entitlement rates that specify minimum manning levels for IRs, all categories are undermanned to various degrees, forcing IR-using organizations to contend with fewer people than they expect and at rates that change from assignment cycle to assignment cycle. Thus, a fundamental contribution to undermanning in IRs is tied to undermanning problems throughout the Air Force. Manning challenges result from how various planning elements, IRs among them, are incorporated into sustainment and accession planning. Sustainment planning for future IR authorizations based on the historical numbers of officers filling IR positions (which are below entitlement levels) will only exacerbate undermanning in the future. To help alleviate this chronic problem, we offer the following recommendations:

- **Include IRs in Air Force–wide manpower and personnel analyses**. Addressing persistent manning shortfalls across the Air Force has significant implications for all officer and enlisted career fields. Actions to improve career field manning overall will lessen the reluctance of career field managers to contribute officers to IR positions—at least to the degree that chronic undermanning challenges are addressed. Including IRs in Air Force–wide manpower studies and personnel analyses is one way to more accurately reflect requirements.
- **Examine and address the discrepancies in the student, transient, and personnel holdee (STP) account.** Examining and addressing the differences between estimated and actual numbers of officers in the STP account (who are not available for permanent positions) can have a similar impact on how the Air Force understands and plans for officer manning, and it may help resolve some broader manpower challenges.

Reconcile Authorizations for Institutional Requirements

One opportunity to improve the IR manning process is to validate and reconcile the manpower authorizations for these positions. Based on assessments of historical and current data on how IRs are filled, we identified instances of excessive double-billeting (multiple officers serving in the same position at the same time), persistent vacancies (positions vacant for a significant period—even years), and IR positions that are consistently filled by the same career field. Validating and reconciling authorizations is likely to reduce the demand for IRs and therefore reduce the number of positions that career fields are required to fill. Actions aimed at reconciling authorizations will help ensure that authorizations are valid and that officers assigned to IRs meet the qualifications of the position; they can also be used to identify true experience and career field requirements in IR-using organizations, and help obviate criticisms about the validity of existing positions. To this end, we offer the following recommendations:

- **Have the AFPC monitor instances of double-billeting** and require IR-using organizations to adjust their authorizations to reflect the true requirements.
- **Eliminate persistent vacancies**. With AFPC oversight, IR-using organizations should validate or eliminate authorizations that have been persistently vacant.
- **Shift IR positions to core Air Force Specialty Codes (AFSCs), where relevant**. IR-using organizations should identify for potential transfer to core AFSCs positions that have been filled over time by officers from the same core AFSC and that IR-using organizations believe would benefit from the expertise of a particular career field.

Expand the Pool of Officers Available for Filling Institutional Requirements

There are other potential courses of action that could reduce the impact of IRs on already-undermanned career fields while still meeting institutional needs. The first is to extend individuals' time in certain positions. There are occasions when individual officers may prefer to remain in a particular type of IR position rather than return to their career field. While extending these individuals does not increase the number of officers overall, there can be benefits to the Air Force by allowing them to do so. Our analysis revealed that officers remain in an IR position for multiple tours about 38 percent of the time.

Another option for expanding the pool of officers is to consider using fourth-year lieutenants (first lieutenants with more than one year in grade and thus three years total as a lieutenant—second and first lieutenant combined) to fill IR positions designated for captains. With a 95-percent opportunity for promotion to captain, most of these officers will be promoted while in the IR assignment and will have a similar level of qualification or experience as newly promoted captains. Opening positions to fourth-year lieutenants will increase the number of officers available to fill IRs without decreasing personnel quality or affecting the operations of the core career fields.

The following recommendations would offer a more deliberate approach to expanding the pool of available officers:

- **Offer opportunities for officers to extend in IR positions**. We recommend that AFPC develop and monitor a process for reviewing requests from officers to extend in IRs. The process should include agreement from the officer's career field and from the commander where the officer is currently assigned to ensure that the officer's performance warrants the extension.
- **Make fourth-year lieutenants eligible for IR positions authorized for O-3s**. Similarly, we recommend that AFPC assignment teams alter their processes to allow O-2s who have completed their fourth year of service to be eligible for IR positions with an authorized grade of O-3—significantly expanding the pool of officers who can fill these positions.

Consider Alternative Workforce Options

There is little official documentation or justification as to why IR positions require an active-duty officer. We believe there are viable alternatives to filling these positions that might be less taxing for the active-duty force, such as using civilians, guard and reserve officers, or contractor personnel. There are two important caveats that will accompany any attempt to expand the workforce beyond active-duty personnel. The first is that while alternative workforce options will reduce the pressure on active-duty career fields to fill IR positions, they will not necessarily be less expensive for the Air Force. Additional study is needed to determine the financial implications of such decisions across the different types of IR positions and locations. A second essential consideration is that, if the alternative workforce options that are pursued involve increasing civilian, guard, or reserve presence to reduce the demand for officers, entitlement rates must be reevaluated at the same time, and leadership must be committed to enforcing them. Otherwise, if the requirement for officers is reduced and manning rates remain unchanged, current manning shortfalls would persist. Still, creative use of personnel other than active-duty officers is a valid consideration for filling IR positions. We offer the following recommendations if the Air Force considers this approach:

- **Provide formal, validated justifications as to why officers are needed in IR positions**. Valid justifications are needed as the basis for evaluating alternative workforce options. Without a clear understanding of requirements, it is not possible to determine whether other personnel can effectively fill some IR positions.
- **Consider using guard, reserve, civilian, and contractor personnel to fill positions in certain IR categories.** Not every IR position is suitable for these alternatives. But there are many circumstances in which guard, reserve, civilian, or contractor personnel can effectively perform the duties and effectively meet mission requirements. Being open to alternative workforce arrangements offers an opportunity to reduce the number of IR positions that have to be filled by traditional career fields.

Address Stigma Surrounding Institutional Requirements

Many IRs face a cultural stigma that has arisen from perceptions that these assignments are "career killers," especially for field-grade officers. The stigma associated with IRs is not universal across all such positions. Senior leader support and strategy positions, for example, are highly sought after and fairly competitive, but many others suffer from some degree of stigma. To change negative cultural attitudes, we recommend the following:

- **Address the real or perceived effects of an IR assignment on officer development**. Making officers aware that IRs will not have a negative effect on their career and ensuring that this is indeed the case will help reverse negative perceptions. In doing so, officer assignment teams may be more likely to send higher-quality officers to these positions, when appropriate. Approaches could include messages from senior leaders emphasizing the importance of IRs, senior leader directives to promotion boards regarding IRs, and, more broadly, an in-depth look at the current and historical impact of IR assignments on promotion rates.
- **Develop education and training into a distinct officer competency**. By professionalizing the academic and training career path, officers with an interest in teaching could pursue their career goals in a more systematic fashion.

Adopt a Centralized Management Structure

Unlike core career fields, IRs have no centralized management structure. There is no equivalent of an assignment team or career field manager to match available personnel to positions, to track positions that are consistently unfilled and evaluate whether the requirements are still valid, to track positions filled by officers from a single career field, or to systematically review and revise entitlement rates to reflect current requirements. The lack of a career field manager may contribute to cases in which IR-using organizations are assigned personnel who are not qualified to fill the positions. Moreover, there are few checks and balances in determining position qualifications. By creating some form of centralized management and responsibility for all IRs, the Air Force could help resolve these deficiencies in the current process. Therefore, we recommend the following:

- **Centralize management of IRs with a career field manager–equivalent who can perform the myriad functions of traditional career field managers**. An IR career field manager would ensure that needs and priorities are accurately represented and that the most appropriate and qualified officers are matched to positions. Such an individual could help remove some of the stigma around IRs, as he or she would be able to weigh the career effects of particular positions and recommend the best career options for available personnel. The individual assigned to this position would have the following responsibilities:
  - **Prioritize and revalidate IR entitlement rates**. As long as manning shortages persist, entitlement rates provide a systematic way to distribute scarce resources. However, they must reflect corporate priorities and be realistic in terms of actual

manning. Existing IR entitlement rates have not been updated since 2001, and it is likely that they no longer reflect current priorities in some cases.

- **Permanently allocate a minimum number of IR quotas, by number and type, to each career field.** If IR requirements are more predictable for career fields, they can be incorporated into accession and sustainment planning and will ensure that a diversity of career fields will be represented across IR organizations. The quota could be a set number or a percentage of the career field authorizations.

Final Thoughts

This study examined the Air Force IR specialties in detail with the aims of identifying how longstanding undermanning could be improved and whether the impact of filling these positions could be lessened for traditional career fields while ensuring that the IR-using organizations are staffed with the qualified personnel they need. The Air Force can pursue many strategies to achieve these goals, and some are very tactical in nature. They could be considered normal housekeeping tasks that should be carried out on a regular, periodic basis, such as eliminating positions that are persistently vacant and those that are no longer valid requirements. But others are far more pathbreaking, such as converting some categories of IRs into their own career field or dramatically changing the management of IRs by appointing an individual to serve as a career field manager.

What this diversity of options illustrates is that there is no silver-bullet solution to lessening the impact of IRs. These requirements will persist and are necessary. While there are many opportunities to improve the process, there is no single, one-size-fits-all action that will solve every related manning challenge. To be sure, appointing a career field manager for this disparate set of specialties would bring more order and oversight than exists today. It would provide a focal point whereby requirements and entitlement rates could be regularly reviewed and revalidated. It would also give someone responsibility for considering the career effects of serving in these positions and taking steps to reduce the stigma that surrounds these assignments. But even that individual and his or her staff will have to take a very deliberate look at each IR category to identify the best courses of action to improve outcomes. In addition, because the challenges with IRs are fully wrapped up in Air Force–wide manning issues, even implementing the full sweep of these recommendations will have a limited effect in mitigating the problem. Ultimately, the challenges associated with filling IRs will be resolved fully and sustainably only when a broader solution to Air Force–wide manpower shortfalls has been implemented.

Acknowledgments

We are grateful to many people who were involved in this research. In particular, we would like to thank our Air Force sponsors Maj Gen Martin Whelan (AF/A3S) and Brig Gen Brian Kelly (AF/A1P) and action officers Col Stuart Pettis and Maj Jason Adams for their help and guidance throughout this study. We are also grateful to the staff at the Air Force Personnel Center, including Robert Cronin and members of the various officer assignment teams who helped us understand the philosophy, management, and execution of the IR processes. We appreciate the information provided by the various staffs of the IR-using organizations, including the leadership and faculty at Air University; representatives from the Office of the Under Secretary of the Air Force, International Affairs; and the staff of Air Force Education Command, including the Air Force Recruiting Service. We appreciate the time and candidness of all the Air Force career field managers who provided detailed information on their science, technology, engineering, and mathematics requirements. This research would not have been possible without their contributions.

This research benefited from helpful insights and comments provided by several RAND colleagues, including John Crown and Ray Conley. We also thank Barbara Bicksler for her contributions to this study and our reviewers, Daniel Ginsberg and Albert Robbert, for their thoughtful comments that greatly improved this report.

Abbreviations

AETC	Air Education and Training Command
AFPC	Air Force Personnel Center
AFRS	Air Force Recruiting Service
AFSC	Air Force Specialty Code
C2	command and control
DoD	U.S. Department of Defense
FAO	foreign area officer
FY	fiscal year
JROTC	Junior Reserve Officers' Training Corps
IR	institutional requirement
PAF	RAND Project AIR FORCE
PAS	political-military affairs specialist
RAS	regional affairs specialist
ROTC	Reserve Officers' Training Corps
STP	student, transient, and personnel holdee
USAFA	United States Air Force Academy
U.S.C.	U.S. Code

Chapter One. Introduction

In an era of force reductions and shrinking military budgets, core U.S. Air Force career field managers and personnel continue to feel the effects of prolonged undermanning. Most career field managers are unable to fully man their associated authorizations and are acutely aware of additional requirements that further reduce their available manpower pool. One significant source of these additional requirements is *institutional requirements* (IRs). IRs are valid, funded manpower requirements that do not align with a traditional, functional career field but are needed to support the Air Force institution—positions such as recruiters, instructors at accession sources, and generalist staff officers. In general, officers from any career field can fill an IR position, though there are exceptions for some IR positions with unique educational or experiential requirements.

Because they lack a formal career field manager and are often seen as a lower priority than operational career fields, IRs will be increasingly difficult to fill if the manpower system becomes less disciplined and competition for manpower intensifies. Space and cyber career field managers believe that the impact of IRs on their ability to man their core authorizations is serious enough to warrant formal study. Thus, Air Force leadership in the offices of the Deputy Chief of Staff, Operations (AF/A3) and the Deputy Chief of Staff, Manpower, Personnel and Services (AF/A1) asked RAND Project Air Force to examine the Air Force's institutional requirements and help determine whether there is a better way to source, manage, and man these service needs in the future.

This report presents our assessment of the IR system, addressing some of the unique challenges that arise in filling particular categories of IRs, and offers recommendations and alternative models for how these corporate requirements might be staffed in the future. In developing these recommendations, we examined and drew on approaches used by the other military services and in the private sector to meet similar corporate needs.

The data for these assessments and recommendations come from a variety of sources. Very little of the information on the IR process at any level is officially documented, so the descriptions of the current status of IRs and the challenges in filling these positions largely derive from discussions with key stakeholders, including officials at the Air Force Personnel Center (AFPC), numerous IR-using organizations, career field managers and other Air Force personnel offices at various levels, and the equivalents of these offices in the other services. We obtained data on current and historical IR authorizations and manning from AFPC. Assessments from industry are from secondary-source literature and consultations with experts in the field.

We begin the next chapter with an overview of the process by which IR positions are filled, a description of the various types of IR positions, and an overview of current and historical trends in filling these positions. Chapter Three explores the general challenges common to all categories of IRs and recommendations for how to mitigate these challenges. Chapter Four examines categories of IRs that have unique attributes and offers tailored approaches to improve manning and decrease the impact of these IRs on career fields. Chapter Five identifies a number of themes that emerge when considering the many recommendations, options, and alternatives discussed in the report. An appendix provides a comprehensive account of manning levels for core career fields as of fiscal year (FY) 2015.

Chapter Two. Institutional Requirements Overview

An important characteristic of IRs is the lack of strategic oversight that determines and prioritizes functional community requirements in a traditional career field structure. In traditional career fields, this strategic oversight and management is the responsibility of functional authorities (general officers and members of the Senior Executive Service serving as deputy chiefs of staff or assistant secretaries), functional managers (senior leaders, designated by the appropriate functional authority, who have day-to-day management responsibility for specific functional communities), and career field managers (day-to-day advocates for their functional community who address issues and specialty concerns across various staffs) (Air Force Instruction 36-2640, 2011).

Because there is no traditional career field structure, IR positions must be filled through alternative means—namely, through a *tax and draft* process. During three assignment cycles (spring, summer, and fall), functional career fields are called upon to fill these positions with a certain number of officers.[1] Career field assignment teams are often reluctant to give up their personnel, especially if they are unable to fill all the positions within their career field. At the same time, organizations that own these positions, which we refer to as *IR-using organizations*, require these officers and may struggle to perform their missions when these positions go unfilled. There is a perception among career fields that the "burden" of filling IRs has increased in recent years, especially with cuts to Air Force end strength, and that filling these positions limits their ability to fill their own required positions by an even greater degree than in the past.[2]

In general, career field managers prioritize the order in which their positions will be filled according to three categories: *must fill*, *priority fill,* and *entitlement fill*. Officers are assigned to must-fill positions first; these officers are typically the best qualified for that specific position. Next, officers are assigned to priority positions, some of which may go vacant, depending on the overall manning of the particular functional career field or the availability of officers with the appropriate grade or experience. Finally, positions designated as entitlement fills are assigned to the remaining available officers based on the entitlement rate for those positions. The *entitlement rate* is the percentage of the entitlement positions that can be filled with the remaining available officers. If a career field has 500 positions for O-3s that are entitlement fills but only 300 O-3s are available after the must-fill and priority-fill positions are assigned, then 60 percent of the O-3

---

[1] While there is a process for how IRs are filled, there is no associated Air Force instruction that outlines or codifies that process.

[2] For more on the impact of institutional requirements on the space career field at the enterprise and individual levels, see Rothenberg et al., 2017.

positions at organizations that own these entitlement fills will actually have an officer assigned to them. The other 40 percent will go vacant. In addition, assignment teams must provide officers to fill IR positions that have been designated to their career field, even as some career field positions remain vacant.

Recognizing this emerging tug of war between IRs and functional career field positions—and the likelihood that it would persist—in 2001, Air Force senior leaders applied the same prioritization scheme to IRs as a way to address manning shortfalls (Headquarters U.S. Air Force, 2001). They designated types of IRs as must-fill, priority-fill, or entitlement-fill positions. Since virtually any officer is qualified to fill an IR position, the entitlement rate for a particular IR applies across the Air Force to all IR-using organizations (rather than to a specific career field). An entitlement rate for a specific type of IR is the percentage of those types of positions that an IR-using organization is entitled to have filled once the rate is set. In reality, an IR-using organization may receive less than the entitlement rate if career fields do not contribute sufficient officers—either because no qualified officers are available or because the rates are not enforced. Moreover, personnel policy and execution stakeholders consider the IR entitlement rates obsolete because they have not been updated since 2001—unlike career field prioritization, which is updated and validated annually.

The following sections describe in more detail the process that the Air Force uses to fill IR positions, the resulting distribution of IR positions and entitlement rates, and an analysis of how IR positions are currently and have historically been filled.

The Institutional Requirement Tax and Draft

Lacking a career field–like structure to address institutional requirements, the Air Force developed unique processes to manage and fill IR positions, in which functional career fields are *taxed* to provide officers to fill IR positions. Three times a year, IR-using organizations (e.g., various schools at Air University, recruiting squadrons) submit requests to AFPC to fill IR positions that are projected to be vacant. AFPC applies the relevant entitlement rates to each set of requests and removes positions over and above that rate. The pool of positions that go on to the next stage of the process are considered must-fills, because they are required to bring each type of IR position to its minimum entitlement rate. After this initial review, AFPC divides the must-fill requirements that can be filled by nonrated officers proportionally among the nonrated career fields based on a formula that accounts for career field size, health, and current contributions to IRs.[3] Because of the natural cycle of personnel moving in and out of positions,

---

[3] The process discussed here and in the remainder of this report applies to nonrated career fields only. Rated officers also fill IR positions, but often in much lower percentages and through a different process than that used for nonrated career fields. There are six ways that a rated officer can be assigned to an IR position: (1) a regional affairs strategist/political-military affairs strategist position that has been designated for a rated officer, (2) the command selection process, (3) an air officer commanding at the United States Air Force Academy (USAFA), (4) selection by

changing demands from using organizations, and variations in each career field's health and current contribution, the number of positions assigned to any given career field can vary widely from one cycle to the next.

After AFPC allots to each career field the number of institutional positions that it must fill, specific positions are distributed through a randomized *draft*, in which officer-assignment teams sequentially select positions that they believe best benefit their career field—because these positions match their available personnel, provide some developmental benefit, or align with a particular priority. The officer-assignment teams then assign officers to fill the positions.

Theoretically, the positions that make it to the draft must be filled by the career fields to which they are assigned. Realistically, though, many career fields cannot fill all of their assigned positions due to undermanning or a lack of qualified personnel, especially in the case of requisitions that have stringent academic or experience requirements. Moreover, the draft process involves a significant amount of gamesmanship. Assignment teams often pick assignments that are easy to fill (e.g., a good assignment location) without regard for how important it is to fill those positions, or they intentionally select positions with stringent academic or experience requirements that they might not be able to fill (thus reducing the number of personnel they will ultimately commit to fill IR positions).

Although the process may sound straightforward, it creates challenges for the career fields assigned to fill IRs. First, it is difficult to incorporate IR positions into career field sustainability planning, because the career field tax is recomputed each assignment cycle and the number of IR positions assigned to a given career field can vary widely from one assignment cycle to the next. A second challenge for career fields is the loss of personnel, especially in undermanned career fields, highly technical career fields (for which a tour outside the career field may lead to a severe degradation of skills), or career fields with significant grade imbalances between personnel and positions. In these cases, losing personnel to fill IRs makes it even more difficult for assignment officers to fill core authorizations associated with a career field. Finally, there is the stigma associated with IR positions—a perception that being assigned to some of these positions has a negative impact on an officer's career. In some cases, these positions are even viewed as career-ending.

The process also creates challenges for IR-using organizations. In May 2015, AFPC estimated that the career fields would fill only 80 of more than 200 IR positions assigned during that cycle. To help ensure that the most important positions were filled first, AFPC asked IR-using organizations to prioritize their submissions, creating, in effect, a "must-must-fill" list for

---

a senior officer, (5) an internal fill within an organization, or (6) through the normal assignment process when the requirement has a high enough priority. Rated officers are used less frequently to fill IR positions because of the number of flying hours they need to meet their experience gates and to qualify them to fill operational duty flying requirements—phase points that have accelerated over the years. Nevertheless, each IR filled by a rated officer translates to one fewer IR that has to be filled by a nonrated officer.

the draft process. However, with more than 120 positions prioritized in this category, many of the top-priority positions were likely to remain vacant. From the perspective of the IR-using organizations, chronic undermanning makes it difficult to perform their missions. Even more problematic is that using organizations may be assigned officers who are not qualified for the vacant position but whom they must keep and use regardless, because they are not likely to get replacements. This mismatch of people and positions can be particularly troubling for positions at accession sources and for instructor positions at premier professional military education locations. The next section defines these IRs more precisely and examines their historical manning.

Institutional Requirement Positions

IRs are a varied set of authorized manpower positions with different needs and challenges. According to the Air Force's Force Management Policy Directorate (AF/A1P) and AFPC, the following is a full account of IR Air Force Specialty Codes (AFSCs), reporting identifiers, and special-duty identifiers:[4]

- 16FX, regional affairs strategist (RAS)
- 16GX, operations staff officer
- 16PX, political-military affairs strategist (PAS)
- 16RX, planning and programming
- 30C0, support commander
- 80C0, USAFA cadet squadron commander
- 81C0, training commander, Officer Training School
- 81T0, instructor
- 82A0, academic program manager
- 83R0, recruiter
- 85G0, Honor Guard
- 86M0, operations management
- 86P0, command and control (C2)
- 87XX, inspections
- 88A0, aide-de-camp
- 91C0, commander
- 97E0, executive officer.

Only positions from O-1 to O-5 in these specialties are counted as IRs; O-6 requirements and assignments are managed by a completely separate organization and process. As stated earlier, we analyzed IRs filled by nonrated line officers. (Only in rare circumstances do non-line officers

---

[4] See the *Air Force Officer Classification Directory (AFOCD): The Official Guide to the Air Force Classification Codes* (Air Force Personnel Center, 2014) for a summary of the duties, responsibilities, and qualifications for these specialties.

fill IRs.) In addition, our analysis excluded a number of specialties from the previous list because they are competitive, high-profile assignments that are always filled: support commander (30C0), commander (91C0), and Honor Guard (85GX).

To simplify our analysis and the presentation of our results, we combined the remaining IRs into several categories based on shared traits. Thus, our analysis focused on the following categories of IRs:

- strategy (16FX, 16PX)
- operations staff (16GX, 16RX)
- accession source command (80C0, 81C0)
- academic instruction and management (81T0, 82A0)
- recruiting (83R0)
- operations C2 and management (86M0, 86P0)
- inspections (87XX)
- senior leader support (88A0, 97E0).

Authorizations for this subset of IRs have held fairly steady (as a percentage of the force) over the past decade and a half, accounting for 6.5–7 percent of total officer authorizations, despite a decrease in total authorizations (Figure 2.1).

Figure 2.1. Authorized IR Positions, FYs 2001–2014

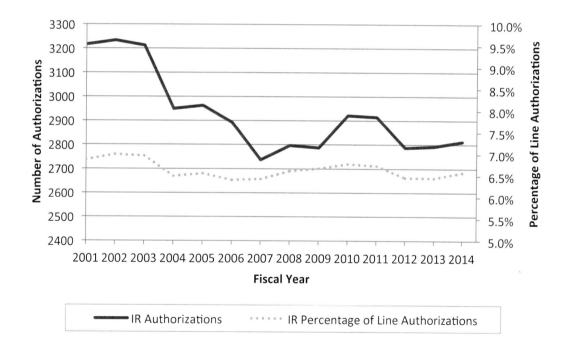

NOTE: Includes authorizations for grades O-2 through O-5 and excludes the commander, support commander, and Honor Guard IRs.

The manning rates in Table 2.1 reflect the aggregate number of authorized positions and assigned officers, as well as entitlement rates and actual manning rates as of the end of FY 2014. The table shows that several categories of institutional requirements are manned below their entitlement rates. These categories include academic instruction and management (81 percent), strategy (64 percent), operations C2 and management (55 percent), inspections (55 percent), and, to a lesser degree, accession source command (99 percent).

Table 2.1. IR Manning, End of FY 2014

IR Category	Authorized Positions	Assigned	Entitlement Rate (%)	Manning Rate (%)
Academic instruction and management (81T0, 82A0)	912	738	98	81
Operations staff (16GX, 16RX)	609	390	59	64
Strategy (16FX, 16PX)	494	427	100	86
Senior leader support (88A0, 97E0)	313	319	Internal fill	102
Operations C2 and management (86M0, 86P0)	142	78	Internal fill	55
Accession source command (80C0, 81C0)	119	118	100	99
Recruiting (83R0)	117	127	100	108
Inspections (87XX)	107	59	Internal fill	55

NOTES: Entitlement rates for the academic instruction and management and the operations staff categories are proportional amalgamations of the entitlement rates for each of the positions within those categories. For example, most 81T0 positions are at 100-percent entitlement, while a few are at 90 percent, and 82A0 positions are at 75 percent; the 98-percent entry for the category is based on the proportion of each position type within the category. Similarly, the 59-percent entitlement rate for operations staff is derived from a 65-percent rate for 16RX positions and a 55-percent rate for 16GX positions.

Chapter Three. Reducing the Impact of Institutional Requirements

There are many opportunities to improve the IR process that can lessen the impact on the career fields that must fill these requirements. These potential reforms can benefit both the using organizations and the career fields that must supply individuals to fill the positions. In general, most of these reforms have some application to all categories of IRs. This chapter examines the broad challenges to manning IR positions and offers recommendations for how IR processes could be improved; the next chapter takes a more in-depth look at how these recommendations can be applied to the specific IR categories listed in Chapter Two.

We acknowledge that the first issue we raise—Air Force–wide undermanning—is not particular to IRs, but it does have a direct effect on why career field managers often find it so difficult to fill IR positions. Thus, we believe it provides important context for the remaining topics discussed in this report.

Address Overall Air Force Undermanning

A major challenge common to all IRs is the systematic, long-term undermanning of funded authorizations. Every IR position is validated by the IR-using organization and funded by the Air Force before it appears in the unit manpower document as an authorization. Despite entitlement rates that specify minimum manning levels, most categories of IRs are undermanned to various degrees, as illustrated in Table 2.1 in Chapter Two. Even must-fill positions in IRs with 100-percent entitlement (such as accession, recruiting, and strategy) may not always be filled, forcing using organizations to operate with fewer personnel than they expect and at inconsistent manning rates from assignment cycle to assignment cycle.

Undermanning of IRs is tied to and exacerbated by larger Air Force manning problems. Two factors drive this mismatch across the Air Force. The first is that major commands often have extra positions in their unit manning documents beyond what they are allocated, a result of budget constraints. At present, there is not enough funding or personnel to fill all the jobs that the service has identified, leaving the Air Force with fewer officers than positions.

The second problem is that students, transients, and personnel holdees (STPs) are chronically underestimated by a substantial amount. STPs are officers who are not available to fill jobs because they are in training, enrolled in long-term education programs, in the process of moving from one position to another, or not available for medical reasons (Air Force Instruction 38-204, 2015). The Air Force anticipates that 9 percent of its officers will be in STP status each year; however, in reality, it is 13 percent or more. The net result is that the Air Force is faced with significantly more officers in STP than planned and too few available officers to fill all the authorized positions, including IRs. While a full assessment of STPs and their impact on the Air

Force was beyond the scope of this analysis, the discrepancy between the estimated and actual STP numbers translates into thousands of personnel, and the manning and operational implications of that difference suggest that it should be a priority for Air Force leaders to resolve.

Additionally, at the career field level, manning for IRs is compounded by the way these positions are incorporated into sustainment and accession planning. Sustainment models determine how many officers should be accessed each year to sustain career field demands for personnel in each grade (to produce enough officers at each grade over a 20-year career). One could argue whether the basis for calculating sustainment should be funded authorizations or validated *entitlement* rates. Unfortunately, current sustainment models use neither to credit a career field for the effect of IR demands. Rather, historical IR *fill* rates over the previous five years are used to credit career fields for their contribution to IRs in the sustainment calculus for the career fields. In other words, because IR positions have been historically manned below their entitlement rates to begin with, using historical fill rates instead of projections of future IR needs creates a self-perpetuating cycle of undermanning. The appendix shows manning for nonrated line AFSCs—the number of officers available to fill positions, given that there are officers in each AFSC in STP status and serving in IR positions. The aggregate manning for grades O-1 through O-5 in these nonrated line AFSCs is approximately 93 percent.

Similarly, IRs are generally not taken into account when considering grade restructuring, force management, and other officer manpower and personnel analyses—but they should be. By leaving IRs out of such assessments, opportunities for reducing grade requirements, deleting lower-priority positions, converting positions to civilian or contracted functions, and other actions that would help alleviate chronic undermanning may be missed.

Recommendations

To help alleviate chronic undermanning, we offer the following recommendations:

- **Include IRs in Air Force–wide manpower and personnel analyses**. Addressing persistent manning shortfalls across the Air Force has significant implications for all officer and enlisted career fields. Still, this shortfall is at the heart of the manpower tug-of-war between career fields and IR-using organizations. Actions to improve career field manning overall will lessen the reluctance of career field managers to contribute officers to IR positions—at least to the degree that chronic undermanning challenges are addressed. Improvements might come from increasing officer end strength or from reducing the number of authorizations. Including IRs in Air Force–wide manpower studies and personnel analyses is one way to more accurately reflect requirements.
- **Examine and address the discrepancies in the STP account.** Examining and addressing the differences between estimated and actual numbers of officers in the STP account (who are not available for permanent positions) can have a similar impact on how the Air Force understands and plans for officer manning, and it may help resolve some of the Air Force's broader manpower challenges.

Reconcile Authorizations for Institutional Requirements

One opportunity to improve the IR manning process is to assess and optimize the IR-using organizations' manpower authorizations. Drawing on assessments of historical and current data on how IRs are filled, we identified instances of double-billeting, persistent vacancies, and IR positions that are consistently filled by the same career field. Reconciling authorizations will not necessarily reduce the demand for IRs, but these inconsistencies indicate that IR authorizations may not reflect the true need for officers in IR-using organizations.

Double-Billeting in Institutional Requirements

Multiple officers serving in the same position at the same time (*double-billeting*) occurs across the Air Force and can skew assessments of career field health and make it difficult to determine what types of officers are needed to fill authorizations. Some double-billeting is understandable, such as when personnel transition in and out of positions. But we were told that, in other cases (especially in IR-using organizations), double-billeting occurs when an inbound officer is underqualified for a particular position and is moved elsewhere in the organization into a position that is already filled by another officer.

AFPC assignment processes consider the number of officers assigned to an organization regardless of the number of positions filled, so this double-billeting does not allow organizations to obtain "extra" officers beyond their entitlement. Rather, it suggests that the authorizations in IR-using organizations do not accurately reflect the types of officers needed for the organization to complete its mission. These inaccurate statements of manpower needs may be one reason for the suggestion we heard from career field managers and assignment teams that IR-using organizations' positions needed to be validated. As a result of double-billeting, fill rates cannot be used as an indicator of whether an organization has enough officers to meet its mission requirements.

In FY 2014, higher-than-average double-billeting was concentrated in the O-4 and O-5 grades and occurred primarily in positions for inspections, senior leader support, and, especially, recruiting. Double-billeting rates for IRs, however, are not any higher than for Air Force positions overall, as indicated in Table 3.1. In FY 2014, there were 220 excess officers double-billeted in IR positions, compared with 6,649 excess officers double-billeted across the Air Force.[1]

---

[1] An officer is defined as an excess officer if he or she is assigned to a position to which an officer is already assigned. If a position has been double-billeted and there are three officers assigned to it, then there are two excess officers for the position.

Table 3.1. Excess Officers in Positions Relative to Total Positions, by Grade, FY 2014

IR Category	O-2	O-3	O-4	O-5	Total
Academic instruction and management	0 / 5	52 / 644	16 / 183	4 / 80	72 / 912
Operations staff	1 / 5	2 / 47	21 / 213	26 / 344	50 / 609
Strategy	0 / 0	0 / 15	12 / 232	13 / 247	25 / 494
Senior leader support	1 / 5	9 / 82	11 / 121	13 / 105	34 / 313
Operations C2 and management	0 / 4	3 / 60	1 / 44	0 / 34	4 / 142
Accession source command	0 / 6	4 / 57	1 / 55	1 / 1	6 / 119
Recruiting	0 / 0	14 / 80	2 / 9	2 / 28	18 / 117
Inspections	0 / 0	3 / 15	3 / 26	5 / 66	11 / 107
Total, IR positions	2 / 25	87 / 1,000	67 / 883	64 / 905	220 / 2,813
Total, Air Force	1,758 / 8,654	2,937 / 2219,076	1,287 / 14,232	667 / 9,562	6,649 / 54,524

NOTE: Shaded cells indicate rates that are higher than those for the Air Force overall in terms of the number of excess officers divided by the number of total positions.

"Cleaning up" these instances of excess personnel per position may not have a drastic quantitative impact because of the relatively low numbers involved. However, if both IR-using organizations and traditional career fields were held more accountable for double-billeting beyond the allotted windows for inbound and outbound personnel, it would create a more realistic picture of career field health and manpower needs. As it now stands, a review of vacant positions in an IR-using organization does not provide an accurate assessment of the unmet manpower needs for the organization.

There is resistance to the idea of cleaning up this double-billeting—first and foremost because it limits organizations' flexibility to move people to already-filled manpower positions. Organizations move personnel for a host of reasons, including to match authorized grades with an individual officer's grade or to assign officers to other organizations during times of transition. There is also resistance because discipline and oversight requires increased administrative resources (time and people) to update authorizations as organizational needs change over time. While reducing the number of double-billeted positions will not inherently reduce the number of authorizations, it will allow IR-using organizations to clean up their authorizations, gain a clearer picture of their manpower requirements, more easily identify gaps in expertise, and, perhaps, dispel the perception that they need to prove the validity of their requirements.

Persistently Vacant Institutional Requirements

While some positions have multiple officers assigned to them, as discussed in the previous section, others have not had any officers assigned to them for a significant period. We call these *persistent vacancies.* Identifying IR positions that are persistently vacant and evaluating whether the requirement is still valid is another step toward rationalizing IR authorizations. Like double-billeting, persistent vacancies create higher apparent demand when, instead, vacant positions are either not essential or so specialized that filling them with a qualified active-duty officer is difficult. Like double-billeted positions, these positions are relatively few in number. A total of 210 positions (7.5 percent of total IR positions) were both vacant in FY 2014 and had been vacant for more than 60 percent of the time between FY 2001 and FY 2014. As shown in Figure 3.1, the operations staff, strategy, and operations C2 and management categories accounted for the bulk of these persistent vacancies. The higher numbers for the strategy category may be explained by the fact that RAS/PAS programs were new and not yet fully manned. Even without the FY 2014 strategy positions, 165 of the positions that were vacant in FY 2014 had been persistently vacant since FY 2001. Each of these positions should be assessed to determine whether a valid requirement remains or whether they can be removed as authorizations.

Figure 3.1. Persistently Vacant Positions, by IR Category

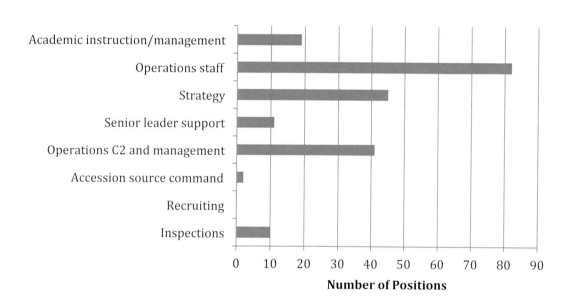

NOTES: The figure shows counts of IR positions that were vacant in FY 2014 and had less than a 40-percent fill rate in FYs 2001–2014 when the position was present in data set. Positions need not be in the data set for each fiscal year. Fill rates are based on number of years the positions were present in data set as of FY 2014.

Specialty-Constant Institutional Requirements

A third option to reconcile the stated manpower requirements for IRs is to identify positions that have consistently been filled by an officer from the same career field over several years. According to our interviews, stakeholders in the career fields and on the Air Staff believe that many IR positions naturally align with particular career fields and that these positions should be "given" to the career fields to fill.

Under such a system, positions would have to be considered on a case-by-case basis to determine whether the IR-using organization is intentionally trying to fill a particular position from a specific career field on a regular basis. Positions that fall into that category could be moved into the career field and managed by the career field managers. This recoding would not reduce the total number of positions Air Force–wide, but it would allow the career fields to incorporate these positions into their routine planning, career development, and accession calculations rather than having to account for them through the more volatile IR process.

Some AFPC officer-assignment teams and IR-using organizations expressed reservations about this approach. Under the current AFPC process and career field prioritization plans, a position converted to a core career field could have a lower fill priority than the same job as an IR position, reducing the likelihood that the position will be filled. However, if the position has consistently been and is currently being filled by individuals drawn from one career field, and if its priority would fall if it were not an IR, the position may need to be revalidated. Among current IR positions, 31 have been consistently drawn from a single career field (Table 3.2).

Table 3.2. Specialty-Constant IR Positions, by AFSC and IR Category

AFSC	Operations Staff	Senior Leader Support	Strategy	Total
Pilot (11XX)	0	0	6	6
Combat systems (12XX)	0	1	0	1
Space operations (13SX)	4	0	1	5
Intelligence (14NX)	1	0	2	3
Cyber operations (17DX)	0	0	2	2
Civil engineer (32EX)	0	1	0	1
Personnel (38PX)	1	2	1	4
Law (51JX)	1	0	0	1
Developmental engineer (62EX)	0	0	1	1
Acquisition manager (63AX)	3	0	2	5
Financial management (65FX)	1	0	1	2
Total	11	4	16	31

NOTE: *Specialty-constant positions* are those that have been filled for at least four years since FY 2001, existed in FY 2014, and had been filled by an individual from the same career field each year they were filled.

These positions are primarily in the strategy, operations staff, and senior leader support categories. The largest contributors to these specialty-constant IR positions are pilots, space operations, combat systems officers, and manpower and personnel. As with instances of double-billeting, these numbers are not high, but, when combined with other strategies, reconciling these authorizations will help reduce the pressure to fill positions through the IR process.

All these options must come with the assurance that a greater effort will be made to fill the remaining IR positions. If the number of IR positions is reduced and fill rates remain steady, IR-using organizations will face a net loss of personnel while still being required to fulfill the same mission. While few AFSCs are manned at their full capacity, senior leaders would have to ensure that revalidated entitlement rates are established and enforced so there is not a disproportionate loss of capacity for IR organizations.

Recommendations

A number of actions aimed at reconciling authorizations will help ensure that authorizations are valid, can be used to identify experience and career field gaps in IR-using organizations, and will help ensure that officers assigned to IRs meet the qualifications for the position. They can also help obviate criticisms that positions are not valid. To this end, we offer the following recommendations:

- **Have AFPC monitor instances of double-billeting** and require IR-using organizations to adjust their authorizations to reflect the true requirements.
- **Eliminate persistent vacancies.** With AFPC oversight, IR-using organizations should validate or eliminate authorizations that have been persistently vacant.
- **Shift IR positions to core AFSCs, where relevant.** IR-using organizations should review positions that (1) have been filled over time by officers from the same core AFSC and (2) that IR-using organizations believe would benefit from the expertise of a particular career field. For IR positions that are considered for transfer to core AFSCs, AFPC could be the broker between the using organization and the career field.

Expand the Pool of Officers Available to Fill IRs

Extend Officers Currently Serving in IR Positions

There are other potential options to reduce the impact of IRs on already-undermanned career fields while still meeting institutional needs. The first is to extend individuals in certain positions. We heard from several career field managers that when officers are assigned to IRs, it is difficult for them to catch up with their peers when returning to their core career fields. Officers with two IR assignments may no longer be qualified for many career field positions requiring significant operational experience. There are occasions when individual officers may prefer to remain in a particular type of IR position rather than return to their career field. Officers who are allowed to remain in their IR assignment are beneficial to the Air Force for the following reasons:

- They are filling a valid requirement.

- They are volunteers and therefore likely to be more dedicated to their duty assignments and more likely to be retained.
- Career field assignment officers do not have to "shoehorn" officers back into the career field if they are less qualified due to serving in IR assignments.
- The career field gets "credit" for the officer serving in an IR.

We reviewed the number of officers who were assigned to an IR position and the rates at which they returned to a core career field (if they stayed in the Air Force). Overall, only 62 percent of officers assigned to an IR who remained in the Air Force returned to a core AFSC. Figure 3.2 shows the percentage of officers who returned to their core AFSC after serving in an IR position. The data suggest that the Air Force should consider allowing some officers to leave their core AFSC and remain in an IR position for multiple tours, since this is already occurring 38 percent of the time. From FY 2000 to FY 2015, 2,924 IR tours ended with the officer returning for another assignment in the same IR, and another 2,026 officers went to a different IR. If only 10 percent of officers returned to any IR position in a subsequent year, it would reduce the number of IR assignments that career fields would have to fill by 52.

Figure 3.2. Percentage of Officers Who Returned to a Core AFSC After Serving in an IR Position, FYs 2000–2014

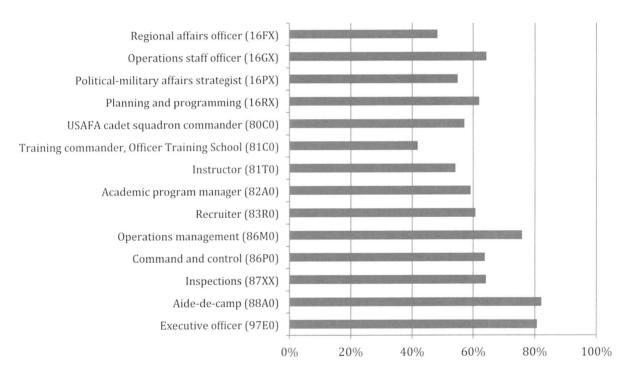

NOTE: The figure includes officers with a rank of O-3 to O-5 who remained in the Air Force after serving in an IR assignment.

Two subsets of officers may be most inclined to remain in particular types of IR positions. First, we found that some IRs are filled by a higher proportion of prior-enlisted airmen than is typically the case in the Air Force as a whole, especially instructor positions (81T0) at Reserve Officers' Training Corps (ROTC) staffs and detachments and recruiter positions (83R0), presumably because they are located in communities where officers prefer to live or near an individual's preferred retirement location. We discuss this topic in more detail in Chapter Four. Allowing personnel who agree to extend their time in the Air Force for one or two years to stay in their last assignment before retiring would reduce the impact of IRs while capitalizing on the experience these individuals have already gained. It also has the added benefit of reducing the relocation and training costs required when filling a position with a new individual. While this option would not be ideal for young officers who are still progressing in their careers, or for those who wish to separate because they are no longer interested in serving in the Air Force (and thus may not be the strongest role models for accessions), it would be ideal for those nearing retirement age. The second subset is officers who serve in IR positions in academic settings at Air University. These officers often require advanced academic degrees to serve in these IR positions, and few in the officer population may have the appropriate credentials. Allowing these uniquely qualified officers to remain in IR positions longer reduces the need to develop new officers and capitalizes on existing expertise and teaching experience.

Allow Fourth-Year Lieutenants to Serve in Institutional Requirements

Another option for expanding the pool of officers is to consider using fourth-year lieutenants (first lieutenants with more than one year in grade and thus three years total as a lieutenant—second and first lieutenant combined) to fill IR positions designated for captains. With a 95-percent opportunity for promotion to captain, most of these officers will be promoted while in the IR assignment and will have a similar level of qualification or experience as newly promoted captains. Opening positions to fourth-year lieutenants will increase the number of officers available to fill IRs without decreasing personnel quality or affecting the operations of the core career fields. Currently, 990 IR positions are authorized at the O-3 grade; more than 60 percent are instructor (81TX) positions. As of the end of August 2015, there were approximately 646 O-3s serving in IR positions (331 in 81TX positions). Including O-2s in their fourth year of service expands the eligibility pool to fill these positions by approximately 2,000 officers.[2]

Recommendations

The following recommendations would offer a more deliberate approach to expanding the pool of available officers:

- **Offer opportunities for officers to extend in IR positions**. We recommend that AFPC develop and monitor a process for reviewing requests from officers to extend in IRs. The

---

[2] Officers with more than three but fewer than four commissioned years of service, counting only nonrated line officers (excluding judge advocate officers).

process should include agreement from the officer's career field and from the commander where the officer is currently assigned to ensure that the officer's performance warrants the extension.

- **Make fourth-year lieutenants eligible for IR positions authorized for O-3s**. Similarly, we recommend that AFPC assignment teams alter their processes to allow O-2s who have completed their fourth year of service to be eligible for IR positions with an authorized grade of O-3—significantly expanding the pool of officers who can fill these positions.

Consider Alternative Workforce Options

Another challenge for analysts attempting to reduce the impact of filling IR positions is that there is little official documentation or justification as to why these positions require an active-duty officer. Without justification, it is difficult to consider viable alternatives to filling these positions that might be less taxing for the active-duty force, such as using civilians, guard and reserve officers, or contractor personnel. While anecdotes abound—and some functions, such as recruiting, are tied to political and legal mandates—there is little written validation of the actual need for officers, and little research has been conducted on the financial and systemic costs and benefits.[3] Therefore, when considering alternative ways to reduce the impact of IRs on career fields, we reviewed numerous other models based on previous attempts to find solutions to similar problems (e.g., the increased use of reservists), current practices already in place in the military (e.g., Junior Reserve Officers' Training Corps [JROTC]), and best practices from academia (e.g., team teaching) and the business community (e.g., outsourcing training and recruiting).

The increased use of reservists to fill various roles previously designated for active-duty personnel has been considered in the past. In 2006, the Center for Strategic and International Studies determined that the services would likely not be able to sustain their levels of operation without drawing substantially and routinely from the reserve component, though it merely offered that conclusion and no effective implementation plan (Wormuth et al., 2006). The following year, RAND released a report addressing funding and chain-of-command challenges associated with integrating reservists into active-duty units on a full-time basis, as well as identifying conditions that make that integration more effective. Many of these conditions centered on culture—specifically, how open a unit is to new members. The research found that integration was easier in environments where the mission set was not technically complex, when positions coincided with reservists' civilian jobs or locations, and when there was not a strong sense of workforce identity, as with pilots, for example (Thie et al., 2007, p. 20). Although the report did not specifically address IR positions, many of them meet the above conditions identified for more successful integration.

---

[3] One exception is a RAND study on the mix of civilian and military faculty at the United States Air Force Academy (Keller et al., 2013).

A later RAND report described several instances in which reservists were well suited to fill active-duty positions, including those with a relatively low operational tempo, those based primarily in the United States, and those with requirements for competencies that may carry over from reservists' civilian jobs (Robbert et al., 2014). There would still be funding and command challenges: The reservists who fill these positions would have to be full-time and would therefore require mandays or statutory tours. But this research suggests that many IR positions could be filled successfully by reserve-component personnel, particularly recruiting, academic, RAS/PAS, and even various staff positions.

Using civilian personnel to fill appropriate IR positions would also reduce the number of IR requirements that the active-duty career fields have to fill and would increase the pool of personnel available to fill those positions. This option would not be practical for all types of IRs, but it might be possible in some academic positions and institutions, where an integrated civilian-officer faculty model that makes use of team teaching could draw on officers to incorporate operational experience into the curriculum as needed. Other options include outsourcing elements of recruiting or allowing civilians to fill staff and managerial roles at recruiting detachments, relying more heavily on civilians in staff and leadership positions, or expanding the JROTC model to ROTC, recruiting, and other areas.

Under this last option, retired personnel would serve in uniform, with their salaries partly covered by the schools and partly by retirement pay, making them a less expensive choice for both the school system and the Air Force than a full-time active-duty officer or full-time civilian. Similarly, newly retired officers would provide a prime pool of qualified and knowledgeable personnel to fill roles within various commands and units and would further bring an element of continuity and experience to the job. More detailed examples of each of these options and IR-specific alternatives are presented in Chapter Four of this report.

Recommendations

We have described a number of options that could increase the pool of available personnel to fill IR positions in various organizations. Two important caveats must accompany any attempt to expand the workforce alternatives beyond active-duty personnel. The first is that pursuing such an approach will reduce the pressure on active-duty career fields to fill these positions, but it will not necessarily be less expensive for the Air Force. Additional study is needed to determine the financial implications of such decisions across the different types of IR positions and locations. A second essential consideration is that, if the alternative workforce options that are pursued involve increasing civilian, guard, or reserve presence to reduce the demand for officers, entitlement rates must be reevaluated at the same time, and leadership must be committed to enforcing them. Otherwise, if the requirement for officers were reduced and manning rates remained unchanged, current manning shortfalls would persist. Still, creative use of personnel other than active-duty officers is a valid consideration for filling IR positions. We offer the following recommendations if the Air Force considers this approach:

- **Provide formal, validated justifications as to why officers are needed in IR positions.** Valid justifications are needed as the basis for evaluating alternative workforce options. Without a clear understanding of requirements, it is not possible to determine whether other personnel can effectively fill some IR positions.
- **Consider using guard, reserve, civilian, and contractor personnel to fill positions in certain IR categories.** Not every IR position is suitable for these alternatives. But there are many circumstances in which guard, reserve, civilian, or contractor personnel can effectively perform the duties and effectively meet mission requirements. Being open to alternative workforce arrangements offers an opportunity to reduce the number of IR positions that have to be filled by traditional career fields.

Address Stigma Surrounding Institutional Requirements

In addition to manpower concerns, many IRs also face a cultural stigma. Some IRs are perceived as "career killers," especially for field-grade officers, but these views differ among the services. The Army, for example, places a high value on instructor positions, whereas individual decisionmakers in the Air Force (notably, those involved with promotion boards) often have a negative view of any tour that takes a person outside his or her primary career field, particularly if that career field is highly technical or operational. Anecdotal evidence suggests that this stigma and the time spent away from one's area of expertise will have a negative effect on an officer's promotion potential, though IR-using organizations insist that a good officer will do well and will be equally considered for promotion regardless of where he or she is serving.

Furthermore, evidence that IRs have a negative impact on promotion rates needs to be balanced with several factors unique to IRs. One is that a disproportionate number of prior enlisted officers choose to volunteer for or are assigned to IR positions, especially in the O-2 and O-3 grades across the range of IRs. These officers are often eligible for retirement at a lower rank than their counterparts and thus often choose these positions to be in a preferred location or job prior to leaving the service. Unfortunately, this forms an association between the IR position and the end of a career.

A second consideration is that some people volunteer for certain positions, such as instructors, because they enjoy the job and would make a career out of these types of assignments if that were an option. These individuals might choose to serve several tours in a teaching position instead of staying on a promotion track in their core career field, again creating the perception that being assigned to an IR position is career-ending. Finally, the perception that IRs are bad for careers becomes a self-fulfilling prophecy, as many career fields send people to these tours who are less likely to be promoted in the first place, reinforcing the stereotype that IRs get in the way of promotions. It is the classic chicken-or-egg argument.

Recommendations

The cultural stigma associated with IRs is not universal across IR positions. Senior leader support and strategy positions, for example, are highly sought after and fairly competitive, but many others suffer from some degree of stigma. To change negative cultural attitudes, we recommend the following:

- **Address the real or perceived effects of an IR assignment on officer development**. Making officers aware that IRs will not have a negative effect on their career and ensuring that this is indeed the case will help reverse the stigma. In doing so, officer assignment teams may be more likely to send higher-quality officers to these positions, when appropriate. Approaches could include messages from senior leaders emphasizing the importance of IRs, senior leader directives to promotion boards regarding IRs, and, more broadly, an in-depth look at the current and historical impact of IR assignments on promotion rates.
- **Develop education and training into a distinct officer competency**. By professionalizing the academic and training career path, officers with an interest in teaching could pursue their career goals in a more systematic fashion.

Adopt a Centralized Management Structure

Unlike core career fields, IRs have no centralized management structure. There is no equivalent of an assignment team or career field manager to match available personnel to positions, to track positions that are consistently unfilled and evaluate whether the requirements are still valid, to track positions filled by officers from a single career field, or to systematically review and revise entitlement rates to reflect current requirements. Without a career field manager, IR-using organizations may be saddled with personnel who are not qualified to fill the positions.

This trend is especially prominent in training and education positions, in which certain education credentials are often required for the school to maintain its accreditation status and offer courses in appropriate subjects. It can also be problematic in recruiting and accession source commands, where certain physical requirements and personal qualities (e.g., extroversion) are beneficial. Recruiting and accession commands also like their positions to be filled by individuals from a variety of career fields so that recruits and trainees are exposed to personnel with a wide range of career field experiences early on.

There is a danger if IR-using organizations place too many restrictive qualifications on a position, as doing so can decrease the likelihood of that position being filled at all or being filled by qualified personnel. Given the current process for assigning IRs, career fields may not have anyone available to meet highly specific qualifications and could intentionally select overly specialized positions that they know they cannot fill to avoid losing officers to an IR. To counter this possibility, IR organizations will often keep requirements to a minimum, which, in turn, increases the risk of being assigned an officer who is underqualified to fill a particular position. This latter alternative is often preferred, however, as these organizations would rather have an underqualified officer than a vacant position.

Recommendations

By centralizing management and responsibility for all IRs, the Air Force could help resolve many of the challenges discussed in this chapter. If the Air Force decides to proceed with such an option, it will also have to consider the role of a functional authority at the general-officer level, the roles and responsibilities for a career field manager compared with other career fields, and the manager's relationship with AFPC and IR-using organizations. The specifics of any such decisions were beyond the scope of this research, but we do recommend that the Air Force consider the following, at a minimum:

- **Centralize management of IRs with a career field manager–equivalent who can perform the myriad functions of traditional career field managers**. Having an IR career field manager would improve accountability on the part of both IR-using organizations and core career fields. A career field manager would ensure that needs and priorities are accurately represented and that the most appropriate and qualified officers are matched to positions. Such an individual could help remove some of the stigma around IRs, as he or she would be able to weigh the career effects of particular positions and recommend the best career options for available personnel. The individual assigned to this position would have the following responsibilities:

  - **Prioritize and revalidate IR entitlement rates**. As long as manning shortages persist, entitlement rates provide a systematic way to distribute scarce resources. However, they must reflect corporate priorities and be realistic in terms of actual manning. Existing IR entitlement rates have not been updated since 2001, and it is likely that they no longer reflect current priorities in some cases.
  - **Permanently allocate a minimum number of IR quotas, by number and type, to each career field.** If IR requirements are more predictable for career fields, they can be incorporated into accession and sustainment planning and will ensure that a diversity of career fields will be represented across IR organizations. The quota could be a set number or a percentage of the career field authorizations.

Overall, IRs could benefit from more explicit and formalized guidance that would codify the Air Force's vision of the functional management of IRs and the relationship between IRs and the career fields, as well as ensure that IRs are more readily tied into larger manpower policies. Guidance could come in the form of a directive from senior leaders, but perhaps the best approach would be codification in an Air Force instruction on IRs, the drafting of which would help bring more visibility to the numerous issues surrounding IRs.

Chapter Four. Assessment of Individual Institutional Requirement Categories

This chapter examines each of the IR categories in depth—identifying the particular challenges of each and offering tailored recommendations. Where relevant, insights from how the other services and industry counterparts organize and manage similar positions inform this analysis.

Strategy: Regional Affairs Strategist (16FX) and Political-Military Affairs Strategist (16PX)

The RAS (16FX) and PAS (16PX) positions were established in the mid-2000s to meet a U.S. Department of Defense (DoD) mandate for all the services to develop foreign area officer (FAO) skills. The Office of the Deputy Under Secretary of the Air Force, International Affairs, manages the two tracks. These positions require international and regional expertise, and officers assigned to these positions serve with the Air Staff, Joint Staff, Office of the Secretary of Defense, unified commands, combatant commands, major commands, and defense agencies and as security cooperation officers or attachés. As of FY 2014, there were 479 O-4 and O-5 validated positions. Figure 4.1 shows total authorized positions, officers assigned, and manning levels. Because these tracks are new, manning with qualified and trained personnel or those in the training pipeline has been increasing steadily, but full manning is not expected until FY 2018. Demand is expected to increase, as currently only about 40 percent of security cooperation officers are trained for RAS or PAS positions. The host units have seen the value of this resource and have asked for more security cooperation officers with this level of qualification.

Unlike many other IRs, the requirements for RAS/PAS positions are quite stringent and, given their high visibility (especially attaché positions), there is strong pressure to ensure that candidates meet them. Both types of positions require at least a master's degree with an international focus from an in-residence graduate school. In addition, RAS candidates must have a high degree of proficiency in a foreign language and at least six months' experience in cultural immersion. The intent of the DoD mandate was for FAOs to have a strong background in an operational career field before serving in an FAO capacity, so candidates are not considered for a RAS position until they have seven to ten years of service or for a PAS position until they have ten to 12 years of service (Air Force Instruction 16-109, 2010).

Figure 4.1. Strategy: Authorized Positions, Assigned Officers, and Manning, by Fiscal Year

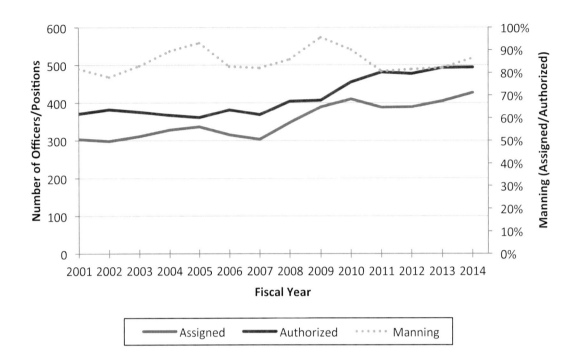

Unlike some of the other services, the Office of the Deputy Under Secretary of the Air Force, International Affairs, does not select its candidates but must rely instead on interested volunteers. Due to the time commitment and education requirements, these positions are not allocated through the IR draft, but career fields that contribute officers do get credit toward their IR tax. Volunteers with extensive language or in-country experience can get waivers from the formal training process, but this is not the primary way people are accessed into the program, nor is the waiver process a straightforward or formalized one.

Because few officers come with the requisite education or language skills, the program must develop about 50 officers a year while incorporating an additional 20 who meet some of the qualifications but need additional training to be fully qualified. Without a waiver or prior expertise, it can take three and a half years for an officer to become qualified, so it is necessary to have two or more officers to fill a single position, as one of those fills is likely to be in training or serving a tour in their primary career field at any given point and therefore physically unavailable to fill an active position. Moreover, the primary career field loses an officer for the development period plus the actual tour length in a RAS or PAS position. Serving in a PAS position involves a single payback tour and essentially functions as a career-broadening assignment. For RAS positions, however, officers are on a dual-track career path, alternating between assignments in RAS positions and in positions in their primary career field for the rest of their career.

The manning rate at the end of FY 2014 was 83 percent for RAS officers and 91 percent for PAS officers, despite an entitlement rate of 100 percent. Higher-profile positions, such as attachés, are generally manned at 100 percent, while less-visible positions are manned at significantly lower levels. Because of pilot manning shortages, fighter pilots are currently restricted from serving in RAS/PAS positions, but host countries often request rated officers for security cooperation or attaché positions. Consequently, 35 percent of filled positions (27.5 percent of authorized positions) have rated officers assigned to them. The Office of the Deputy Under Secretary of the Air Force, International Affairs, may use some of the more than 100 RAS-certified reservists (O-4 to O-6) to make up the shortfalls, but this is only a short-term solution in its current form. Reservists may provide a useful long-term solution, as many may have acquired the necessary educational and language qualifications through their nonmilitary careers, but their use would require a formalized long-term funding structure.

Unlike other IR positions, RAS/PAS positions are more career-friendly for the individual officer. Many officers who meet the stringent requirements are already very competitive and, anecdotally, do well compared with their peers. Many of these positions are viewed as career-enhancing, even if they come at the expense of a squadron command for some officers. One complication, however, is the ability of highly qualified officers from primary career fields to maintain their qualifications, which they may lose during the time spent training and serving in a RAS/PAS position. In these cases, they may require recertification. From the career fields' perspectives, losing people for that long can be detrimental, and some are hesitant to offer up their personnel. The major exception to that rule is intelligence officers, who tend to volunteer and get released in greater numbers because their career field qualifications closely match RAS/PAS requirements. There is little recourse, however, for officers who would like to stay on a RAS career path and specialize in FAO knowledge and skills; unless their career field releases them, they have no option but to bounce back and forth between their core career field and the RAS track.

Parallel Practices: Other Services

The FAO track in the Marine Corps is most like the Air Force's program. The Marine Corps employs a dual-track process (service in the primary career field and participation in the FAO program), but it does not have a PAS or single-tour equivalent. The Army has, by far, the largest number of FAOs and the most-established program. Originally, Army FAOs were dual-tracked like these personnel are in the Air Force and Marine Corps today. In 1997, Army FAOs became a single-track specialty as part of the operations support career field (and would not return to their core career field once accepted to FAO positions). While FAOs may lose direct operational relevance or currency on weapon systems, most officers still have extensive experience from their initial seven to ten years in a traditional career field. The Navy followed the Army's pattern and also has a single-track option, which may limit its officers' ability to maintain operational relevance but increases their expertise and options for promotion and retention within the FAO track (Alrich, Adams, and Biltoc, 2013, pp. 6–10).

Recommendations

To help address undermanning for RAS/PAS positions, we offer the following recommendations:

- **Develop RAS as a single-track career field for interested volunteers.** Many users of Air Force RAS/PAS positions want a rated officer or someone with up-to-date experience on technical systems—making the dual-track RAS or single-tour PAS a good option to maintain. However, for individuals who are interested in pursuing an international affairs career, developing a single-track career field would reduce some of the burden of training new people, develop more professionalized RAS personnel, and reduce the need for other career fields to give up uninterested or underqualified officers as part of the IR process.
- **Make education and training for RAS/PAS officers more accessible.** Developing online graduate degree and language programs or finding cultural immersion opportunities closer to a candidate's home station would allow officers to continue to serve in their core career field while pursuing these opportunities, or at least not have to relocate as far for immersion. These approaches, both of which are currently under consideration by the Office of the Under Secretary of the Air Force, International Affairs, might make career fields less hesitant to allow volunteers to participate.

Aside from a stricter adherence to the must-fill status, other options to improve undermanning for RAS/PAS positions include

- formalizing the waiver process for officers in certain experience categories (e.g., former security cooperation advisers, attachés, Afghanistan-Pakistan Hands program personnel) to shorten the training required to qualify for entry into the RAS or PAS program
- using qualified guard and reserve personnel to fill RAS or PAS positions.

Operations Staff: Operations Staff Officer (16GX) and Planning and Programming (16RX)

Operations staff positions are some of the more difficult to characterize broadly because they are scattered so widely across the Air Force. Officers in these positions serve as operations staff officers (16GX) and planning and programming officers (16RX). Their combined entitlement rate is 59 percent (55 percent for 16GXs and 65 percent for 16RXs). In FY 2014, operations staff positions made up the second-largest category of IRs, with 609 authorized positions. When it came to actual officers assigned, this category was third behind academic instruction and management and strategy, with only 390 assigned personnel. The number of authorized positions has fallen fairly consistently since a high of almost 944 in FY 2001 (Figure 4.2). Manning hit a low of less than 56 percent in FY 2010 but has increased steadily since then to a level of 64 percent at the end of FY 2014. Operations staff positions also have the highest incidence of double-billeting beyond what can be attributed to staff transitions, with ten positions each being filled with at least three people in one year.

Figure 4.2. Operations Staff: Authorized Positions, Assigned Officers, and Manning, by Fiscal Year

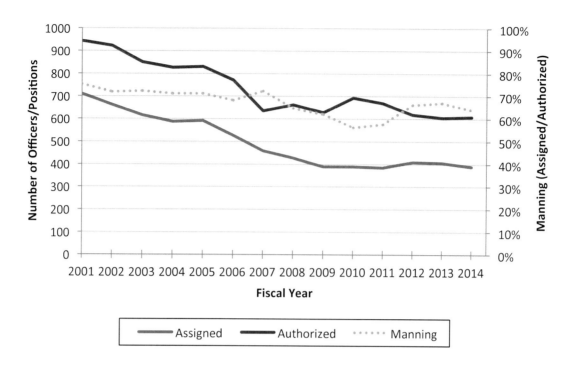

The majority of operations staff positions are for O-5s, but there is a proportionally uneven distribution of manning across the grades, along with some persistent vacancies (Figure 4.3). Operations staff positions have the highest incidence of persistent vacancies, with 82 positions regularly going unfilled that should be revalidated or removed from the books. This IR category also has 11 positions that were consistently filled by the same AFSC (four by space [13SX], three by acquisition management [63AX], one by intelligence [14NX], one by personnel [38PX], one by judge advocate [51JX], and one by finance [65F]). It may be beneficial to convert these positions into the core career fields. Doing so would reduce the overall IR burden filled via the draft, allow these career fields to better plan for filling the positions, and help improve the overall fill rates for 16GXs and 16RXs.

Figure 4.3. Operations Staff: Persistent Vacancies, Assigned Officers, and Authorized Positions, by Grade, FY 2014

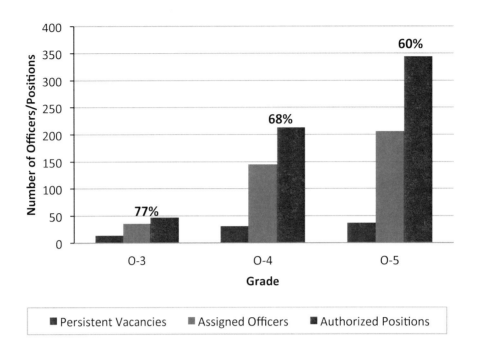

Accession Source Command: USAFA Cadet Squadron Commander (80C0) and Officer Training School Commander (81C0)

Accession source command positions are different from other IRs in that they are command positions at the USAFA and Officer Training School. These officers are responsible for commanding, instructing, evaluating, counseling, and monitoring students during all phases of training. There are currently 119 authorized positions, most at the rank of O-3 or O-4. With a 100-percent entitlement rate, these command positions have a 99-percent manning rate—the third-highest fill rate among IRs. While the total number of positions has remained roughly consistent (Figure 4.4), the manning percentages declined in the early 2000s but drastically improved in 2010, when the manning percentage rose from 61 percent to 94 percent.

There is not much room for reducing or converting 80C and 81C positions, as there have been only two persistent vacancies and no positions consistently filled by officers from the same career field. There is little opportunity to civilianize these positions because of their command responsibilities, but, anecdotally, that makes them more appealing for individual officers. This is especially true for officers in career fields that may not have many functional command opportunities.

Figure 4.4. Accession Source Command: Authorized Positions, Assigned Officers, and Manning, by Fiscal Year

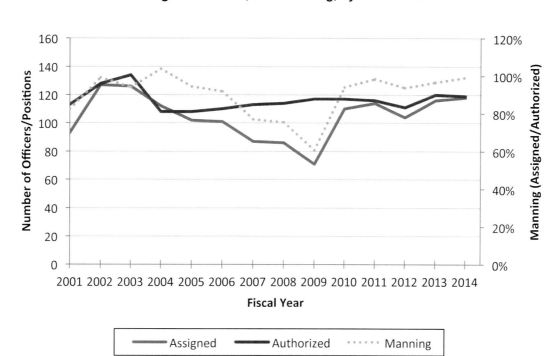

Academic Instruction and Management: Instructor (81T0) and Academic Program Manager (82A0)

Academic instructor (81T0) and manager (82A0) positions involve designing curricula and teaching and managing a wide variety of courseware, primarily located in the different schools at Air University at Maxwell Air Force Base. Together, these positions make up the vast majority of IRs, with 912 authorized positions in FY 2014. Even though most of those positions have a must-fill priority, the fill rate in FY 2014 was only 81 percent. The number of authorized positions has been on a slow decline since FY 2001 (Figure 4.5); however, manning has also declined somewhat, particularly since FY 2010.

There are some grade mismatches between authorized and assigned positions, as Figure 4.6 illustrates. Only O-4 positions are being filled at roughly 100 percent; O-3 positions are substantially undermanned, and there is significant overmanning among O-2s and O-5s. The O-2s are almost entirely serving in O-3 positions (adding further support to the recommendation for using fourth-year lieutenants to fill captain positions), while O-5s are covering a variety of other positions, including seven O-6 positions, 51 O-4 positions, and 26 O-3 positions. There are also 114 O-4s in O-3 positions and 51 O-5s in O-4 positions. While some of this grade mismatching can be explained by promotions, the bulk of it is indicative of Air University's struggle to get an adequate number of officers assigned to its positions. Rated officer fill rates for academic positions are among the lowest for IRs at just 5.4 percent in FY 2014, reflecting the

29

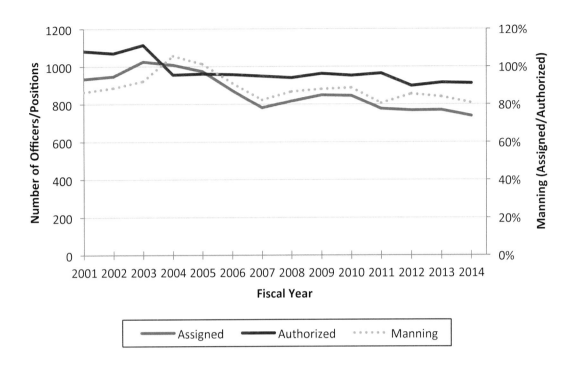

Figure 4.5. Academic Instruction and Management: Authorized Positions, Assigned Officers, and Manning, by Fiscal Year

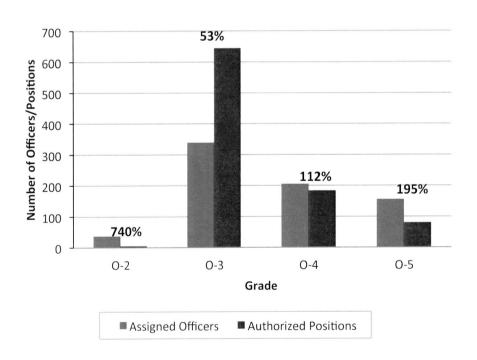

Figure 4.6. Academic Instruction and Management: Assigned Officers and Authorized Positions, by Grade, FY 2014

30

low priority the rated community places on these instructor positions, despite the positions being at some of the most highly regarded Air Force educational institutions.

The cultural stigma against instructing, particularly at Maxwell Air Force Base, is at the heart of Air University's challenge in getting qualified and interested personnel. Such a stigma became apparent to us during discussions with officers throughout the Air Force, officer assignment teams, and even personnel currently leading and working at Air University. More so than any other IR, being assigned as an instructor or program manager at Maxwell is seen as a death knell for an officer's career, especially for those in the field-grade ranks. Leaders at Air University agree that officers assigned to these positions are unlikely to reenter their core career field; this, combined with the fact that it is often nonvolunteers who are sent to fill these positions, turns the perception that an assignment at Air University spells the end of a career into a self-fulfilling prophecy. With the exception of officers who want to teach or are interested in retiring near Montgomery, Alabama, few officers are willing to volunteer for these positions.

Academic positions have an additional complication in that, aside from RAS/PAS positions, they have some of the highest qualification requirements. While a relatively large number of officers have the required master's degree in math, science, or engineering, finding an equivalent number of officers with advanced degrees in social sciences or the humanities can be very challenging. In most cases, these degrees are not merely the schools' preferences but are required for the schools to maintain their accreditation (to issue civilian master's and doctoral degrees).

Career fields often do not have available personnel who meet these qualifications, and since Maxwell positions are usually the last to go in the IR draft, Air University is faced with taking and making use of any officer it is assigned rather than risk getting no one at all. As a result, too often, the schools wind up with mismatches, such as core developmental engineers teaching social sciences, and high rates of prior-enlisted members who may not have the required master's degrees. Furthermore, not every officer is a natural instructor; education and teaching are professional skill sets that civilians often get entire degrees in before teaching. Aside from a basic how-to course (Academic Instructor Course), Air University must rely on many instructors with little or no prior teaching experience in some of its elite schools, and it is further hampered by the high turnover rate (20–30 percent) of its military faculty every year. The career field manager, on the other hand, is losing personnel to positions with little relevance to the core career field and in much greater numbers than for other IRs.

ROTC positions are another subset of academic positions that are significantly undermanned. With 145 detachments that require three officers each, ROTC is currently more than 130 personnel short of its desired manning levels, and nearly every detachment is undermanned. Due to political decisions to keep ROTC detachments open across the country despite a drop in demand, as well as contractual obligations with universities, Air Education and Training Command (AETC) has had to spread its ROTC instructors across detachments. There has been a reluctance to assign civilians to staff detachments because it takes a waiver from the Secretary of Defense to allow civilians to teach (though they can hold staff jobs in place of officers). AETC has tried to employ civilians in administrative roles, but it has been difficult to keep civilians in these positions because of the low pay grade.

AETC has also proposed a model for using recently retired personnel to fill teaching positions, though another consideration would be to implement a JROTC-like model in which retired officers come back in uniform. A similar approach was proposed by RAND in a 1999 report that assessed a series of alternatives for staffing ROTC positions using a combination of active-duty officers, reservists, and former military civilians and relying on civilians to do administrative jobs. The authors estimated that filling these positions with reservists would decrease the need for active-duty personnel by roughly 15 percent, which supports the concept of using a mix of personnel to staff ROTC positions (Goldman et al., 1999).

Alternative Options

Implementing the solutions outlined here may help reduce the number of academic IR positions by a small amount. We found 19 persistent vacancies in the academic positions, so identifying and evaluating the need for those positions would be a start. However, no positions were consistently filled by a single career field. Thus, unless these positions were transferred to a newly created core AFSC (as we discuss later in this section), the remainder would continue to be filled through IR mechanisms.

The greatest gains for reducing the burden of instructor positions would most likely come from alternative workforce options. Air University is investigating several solutions to improve its undermanning and maintain a more qualified workforce. There has been a big push for distance learning, but, with the need for ongoing course design and updates, Air University estimates that this option would require nearly as many people. Another consideration is requiring some developmental education graduates to stay on an extra year to teach. This would ensure a high-caliber faculty officer in the classroom, but career field managers would likely push back against this alternative because it would take their highest-rated officers away from career fields for additional time. There are other options as well, including creating an instructor career field, workforce diversification, and shared-faculty models.

Instructor Career Field

Another potential option is to return to the concept of education officers as a functional area under human resources for those who want to become career instructors. Many officers who wind up at Air University do several tours there, especially those who volunteer, so creating a career path for them to pursue would allow the Air Force to blend their direct operational experience with their teaching expertise in the classroom. In 1954, the Air Force developed a distinct career field for education and training education officers (75XX). A 1991 occupational survey report of the education and training field described the various duties of these officers, as well as those with an education and training special-duty identifier (09XX) that functioned in the same way that academic instruction and management IRs do now (U.S. Air Force, 1991).

At that time, there were 414 officers assigned to the education and training career field and 1,388 officers with the special-duty identifier, meaning that 23 percent of officers involved in education were full-time professionals in the field. Sixty percent of education officers reported that they wanted to stay in their career field, and a third of officers in special-duty positions also indicated they would be interested in continuing on in education and training. Most of the duties for officers in these positions covered the same responsibilities that academic instruction and management IRs cover today, and even at the time, many survey respondents said that experience in education and training was important or essential for many of their tasks.

The study noted that staff positions in educational institutions could be equally filled with officers from a variety of career fields. These positions did not require any degree of expertise, but some level of knowledge of the institution, its mission, and the education process is likely to be more useful for staff officers than none at all.

Reinstituting education officers as a core career field offers an effective way to achieve three aims: (1) improving the quality of instruction and education by retaining experience and developing particular academic areas of expertise, (2) reducing the stigma associated with academic IR positions by developing a career field with its own promotion path, and (3) reducing the number of IR positions that the Air Force as a whole would have to fill via the draft process. Given the numbers of instructor positions and the need to retain operational relevance, some will have to continue to be filled through the IR process, but an education officer career field could significantly reduce these numbers. Initially, many of the positions in such a career field could be filled with officers currently serving in IR positions who have gone into the informal "education track" or would otherwise retire but might consider staying on active duty if they could continue instructing so as to reduce any impact to the other AFSCs. While creating a new career field will not improve overall manning problems, it will reduce the variable demand on other AFSCs associated with the IR tax.

Workforce Diversification

IR-using organizations most often cite operational relevance to justify having officers in the classroom. These officers lend credibility to the courses and allow instructors to add real-life examples of how the course material has influenced their work—one reason why several of the Air University schools prefer to have their graduates return as instructors. Assigning officers to instructor positions can be easily justified for military-specific courses, such as leadership, but it is harder in the case of social sciences or humanities classes. In these latter situations, it might be beneficial to incorporate professional civilian instructors, though the ability to do so may be limited because some schools, such as the Air War College, have external official guidance (that they have petitioned to change) that a certain percentage of their faculty must be active-duty military. Because of these mandates, a change in policy would be required to substantially increase the number of civilians in those positions. A greater use of guard and reserve personnel might also allow the Air Force to access to a larger pool of qualified individuals, as long as there are enough guard and reserve students attending the courses to justify incorporating them.[1]

In a 2013 RAND study of USAFA, the authors offered several recommendations regarding the mix of civilian and military faculty based on a number of variables. Many of those recommendations, which could also apply to Air University and academic positions at military institutions more broadly, include shifting to greater use of civilian faculty, varying the ratios of civilian to military faculty based on the discipline, and relying more heavily on company-grade officers as instructors (Keller et al., 2013, pp. xx–xxi).

Shared-Faculty Models

Shared-faculty or team-teaching models are successfully employed in industry (as discussed later in this section) and have applicability in the Air Force school system. Air University is, in fact, considering a number of shared-faculty models in which civilians with theoretical and subject-specific backgrounds and military personnel with operational experience could be paired to instruct on a particular topic; these teams could then be shared across all the schools at Air University when relevant (rather than having faculty dedicated to a single school, such as the Air War College or Air Command and Staff College). Although it would take time to hire or assign faculty with the necessary expertise, this shared model would, in time, make better use of the military officers because they would be available to provide real-world operational context across the university rather than only within a particular school, where their operational expertise may not be fully utilized.

There are other benefits as well. Team teaching would lessen the need for officers to learn a wealth of theoretical material and subject matter outside their area of expertise. It would create an opportunity for peer-to-peer mentorship for new instructors, a trend seen at universities that employ team teaching to the benefit and satisfaction of junior teachers (Rabb, 2009). Since many officers assigned to instructor positions have little or no formal training in instructional techniques, pairing them with a professional civilian counterpart who could act as a mentor could improve their effectiveness in the classroom.

Air University's Ira C. Eaker Center for Professional Development employs a team-based model that could be more widely adopted across the schools to help reduce demand for active-duty officers as full-time teachers.[2] In this model, civilians provide the vast majority of the

---

[1] This is because, in some cases, reserve component members can be called to active duty for the purpose of organizing, administering, recruiting, instructing, or training reserve-component members and not solely for performing these functions for active-duty members. (See, for example, 10 U.S.C. 12310, 10 U.S.C. 101, and 32 U.S.C. 328)

[2] Located at Maxwell Air Force Base, the center provides multidisciplined technical training and professional continuing education to Air Force and other DoD personnel, as well as international students. The center is made up of five schools: Commanders' Professional Development School, U.S. Air Force Chaplain Corps College, National

instruction on general and theoretical issues. When specific operational topics are covered during instruction, military lecturers (officers currently serving in relevant technical or leadership positions) instruct on these topics for several courses or schools. In this way, a single course has a mix of different instructors who can provide subject-matter expertise, professional teaching experience, and operational relevance. While students might lose some of the potential for after-hours mentorship, the usefulness of which is anecdotal rather than based on research, they would gain access to the most current practitioners who could be invited from a wide spectrum of career fields. At the same time, the full-time civilian academics would benefit from regular and continued contact with these experts, allowing them to keep their courses up to date.

Parallel Practices: Industry and the Other Services

Education in Industry

The majority of corporations spend a great deal of time and energy on training, but most do not provide education, making direct comparisons with a military environment difficult. However, when corporations do focus on training, very few firms pull line managers or operators out of their careers to be full-time instructors. In general, they prefer to utilize training professionals—even if they are in-house—to provide the bulk of the education and training (especially for midlevel- and senior-management development) and bring in workers from other units primarily as guest or part-time lecturers. There have been very few studies on efficacy relative to instructors with operational experience versus professional educators, but a 1979 survey of instructors on the attributes of trainers found that the most important skills for trainers were (1) human relations, (2) communication, (3) knowledge of the training and development field, (4) analytical skills, and (5) management skills. Notably, knowledge of the organization did not make this top-five list; it came in at number six (Dunnette and Hough, 1995, p. 509). One study that examined whether line managers serving as trainers improved the effectiveness of training found that line mangers did not enable higher levels of learning or transfer of knowledge (Perez, 2006), suggesting that using professional instructors is more effective than operationally relevant ones.

Team Teaching in Higher Education

Team teaching has been widely considered to be an optimal educational practice for several decades, especially in technical and business fields in which this approach exposes students to a blend of academic and real-world expertise in the classroom. Few rigorous studies have been carried out to test the efficacy of this approach in providing better learning or work environments for students and practitioners. But the studies that have been conducted stress a number of

---

Security Space Institute, Defense Financial Management and Comptroller School, and the U.S. Air Force Personnel Professional Development School.

different models for team teaching that they have found to be most useful. One model involves the use of paired, full-time faculty with different backgrounds who work together to provide course content from multiple perspectives.[3]

A second model is to rely primarily on a single academic instructor with the heavy use of guest lecturers from industry. A 2007 study of such an approach at a university demonstrated that bringing in experts greatly improved students' applied learning and that an overwhelming majority of the students found the guest lectures both interesting and useful (Rowland and Algie, 2007). This model allowed academics to maintain ties to professionals and allowed the university to bring in the most up-to-date practitioners each term to share their experiences applying their knowledge in practice.

Education in the Other Services

The military services use different models to fill IRs, and in a different education and training culture. Senior personnel officers in the Navy told us that officers view volunteering for this type of shore duty as a way to intentionally cap out their careers at or before retirement age. Those who wish to leave the Navy can take an instructor position and are frequently offered the opportunity to complete a master's degree as part of the deal, allowing them to be more competitive in the civilian world. Instructing is not necessarily viewed as a negative career-ender but instead as an option to transition out of the military. The Marine Corps, on the other hand, has a requirement to fill IR-type roles built into its career progression plan. For this reason, many IR-type jobs in the Marine Corps, including instruction, are simply part of the promotion path with no stigma attached. The Army is unique in that it places a much higher value on formal education, and many instructor positions, especially those that are operationally relevant, are sought after. However, positions that are filled with nonvolunteers (such as ROTC) and positions at the Army War College suffer from similar types of issues as Air University in terms of caliber of personnel and interest or experience in instructing. To balance the lack of active-duty experience and interest in teaching with operational relevance, the Army Command and Staff College at Fort Leavenworth has experimented with hiring newly retired personnel as instructors, though this program is too new to determine its impact on training.

Recommendations

Academic positions are some of the most difficult IRs to fill due to a combination of strict qualification requirements and the stigma associated with these positions because of their apparent career-ending potential. We have offered a wide variety of options that the Air Force could pursue to reduce the impact on traditional career fields in filling these positions. In addition to taking advantage of housekeeping opportunities to reduce the number of positions by

---

[3] See Dong, El-Sayed, and El-Sayed (2011) for an overview of best practices in applying this form of team teaching.

removing persistent vacancies and converting consistent fills to core AFSCs, the most promising approach is to **professionalize instruction by making it a career field function under human resources**. Reinstituting education officers as a core career field offers an effective way to

- improve the quality of instruction and education by retaining experience and developing particular academic areas of expertise
- reduce the stigma associated with academic IR positions by developing a career field with its own promotion path
- reduce the number of IR positions that the Air Force as a whole would have to fill via the draft process.

Given the number of instructor positions and the need to retain operational relevance, an education officer career field could significantly reduce the number of instruction positions to be filled through the IR process.

While an instructor career field provides a career track for a group of "professional military instructors," which will always be needed, **there are still potential savings and efficiencies that can be gained by employing a diverse faculty base** that draws on the guard and reserve, retired military, and civilians to fill instructor positions, as appropriate, across the Air Force school system. To this end, we offer the following recommendations:

- Incorporate guard and reserve instructors into schools with high numbers of guard and reserve students.
- Require graduates of intermediary schools to teach for a year after graduation.
- Develop a shared-faculty model at the Air University schools. Team teaching that includes professional civilian instructors and military personnel with operational expertise is one such approach.
- Increase the overall proportion of civilian faculty, weighed by discipline.
- Rely more on company-grade officers as instructors.

The ROTC program is a unique element of the Air Force "school" system and requires a particularly tailored approach. We believe the most promising solution to improve undermanning in these positions is to **adopt a JROTC or more civilian-intensive model for ROTC positions.** Models in which civilians or retired officers come back in uniform to teach in ROTC detachments may not save the Air Force money, but they would reduce the impact on traditional career fields to fill these positions, with the likely outcome of increasing fill rates.

Recruiter (83R0)

Recruiting both the required number of people and quality individuals has become an increasingly high priority within the Air Force, and the AETC commander has placed specific emphasis on filling recruiting positions within detachments. Although officers in these IR positions are not usually directly responsible for the recruitment process, they do manage the enlisted recruiters and help ensure the success of recruiting organizations. The entitlement rate for recruiter officers is 100 percent, and manning in FY 2014 was 108 percent (Figure 4.7). The leadership of the Air Force Recruiting Service (AFRS) expressed concern about any manning level under 100 percent, and, even at an aggregate rate greater than 100 percent, AFRS still has trouble filling the required positions. Manning levels were below 100 percent from FY 2005 through FY 2010, with a greater than 50-percent increase in authorized positions since 2001, reportedly due to increased demand during the wars. With no persistently vacant positions or positions consistently filled by the same career field, there is little room to remove excess positions.

Figure 4.7. Recruiters: Authorized Positions, Assigned Officers, and Manning, by Fiscal Year

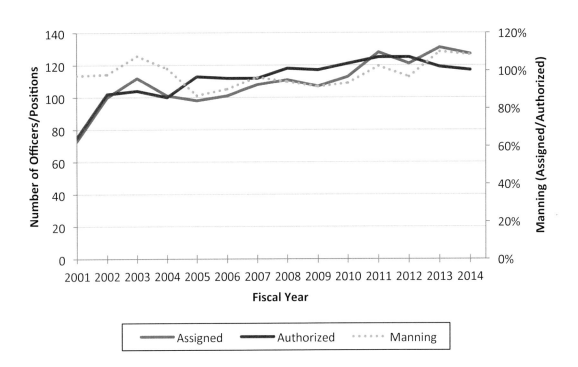

Although the number of recruiter positions has increased, AFRS reports that it has needed to cut down the number of detachments and pull many officers into centralized locations. There are some advantages to this option. Fewer officers are required to act in managerial roles overseeing enlisted personnel, and detachments may be represented by greater occupational diversity with more officers in a single location. While enlisted personnel primarily conduct hands-on recruiting, officers at the detachments are a resource for potential recruits who might have questions about officer careers.[4] For highly specialized fields, such as health practitioners, it is

---

[4] Of concern to AFRS leadership is the fact that the overwhelming majority of officer recruiters come from nonrated career fields. There are only six billets for rated officers—about half as many as in the past—and this small number limits potential recruits' access to rated officers and career fields.

considered helpful to have officers conduct recruiting rather than enlisted personnel because of the shared educational experience officers are likely to have with potential recruits.

As far as positions themselves, officers in recruiter positions generally serve as flight or squadron commanders. Although the majority of authorized positions are for captains, many of them are filled by lieutenants (O-1s) or sometimes majors (O-4s), as shown in Figure 4.8, which creates a grade mismatch between what AFRS requires and what it actually receives.

Figure 4.8. Recruiters: Authorized Versus Assigned, by Grade, FY 2014

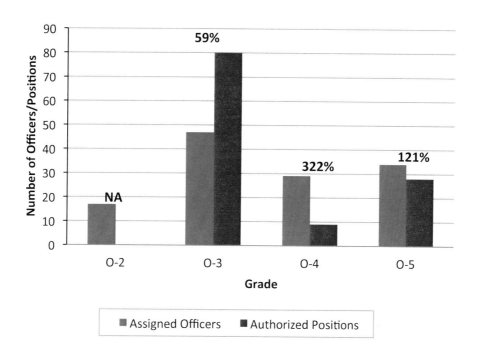

Many career fields and individuals view recruiting positions as less appealing than other IRs, though the Air Force does offer command position alternatives for career fields that have few internal opportunities. Nevertheless, despite such perceptions, many officers have historically volunteered for recruiting positions, and these personnel are often among the first selected by officer assignment teams in the IR draft. These positions also provide an officer with an opportunity to get an assignment in his or her preferred location. This is especially important for prior enlisted officers who are approaching retirement age and may want the opportunity to serve their last tour in the community where they intend to retire, saving on moving costs after leaving the military. Largely because of this opportunity, prior enlisted officers are represented in recruitment positions at much higher rates than the Air Force average for O-1, O-2, and O-3 positions (Figure 4.9).

Although there is little room for reductions in the number of authorized positions, as previously discussed, recruiting positions could benefit from several workforce options, one of which is to allow officers near retirement to extend in place beyond a normal tour length.

Figure 4.9. Recruiters: Rates of Prior Enlisted, by Grade, FY 2014

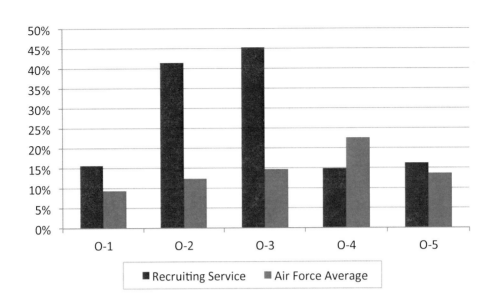

Other options, such as converting positions away from active-duty officers or using guard and reserve personnel, have less chance of success. AFRS leadership does not support converting positions away from uniformed officers to civilians or contractors for two reasons. First, as mentioned previously, officers appeal to a variety of potential recruits because they represent a diversity of career options and a greater degree of affinity to recruits interested in specialty career fields. Second, because many recruiter positions are command positions with responsibility over other military personnel, an officer is best qualified to handle behavioral or Uniformed Code of Military Justice issues. This is particularly true of flight commander positions because having an officer present at smaller locations at all times can help to forestall potential problems in the first place.

In the past, AFRS has used guard and reserve personnel to fill active-duty recruiter positions, primarily with Overseas Contingency Operations funding, which was justified because of the increased recruiting demands stemming from the wars in Iraq and Afghanistan. This option, however, is no longer viable. There has been some thought given to combining active-duty, National Guard, and reserve recruiting stations to pool efforts. But this approach raises different potential challenges, such as increased competition between the different components for recruits and how total force recruiting stations would be funded. AFRS has also considered incorporating more civilians into the recruiter workforce, especially for non-command staff and to help recruit health professionals, but finding appropriate sources of funding under the current system, again, poses difficulties.

Parallel Practices: Industry and the Other Services

Industry Recruiting

Until recently, many large companies outsourced all or part of their recruiting to third parties. Doing so provides a number of benefits to a company, including freeing up human resources departments to focus on their core duties, saving money, improving recruitment quality, and providing recruiting expertise in the newest tools and technologies (Biro, 2013). Additionally, outsourcing to third parties can be a process that is more flexible in meeting year-to-year demand for new recruits. Rather than having a set number of recruiters based on previous assessments of need, which may be too high or low and thus waste resources, a specialized recruiting company can flex more rapidly and could therefore cost less in the long run. There are challenges, however, including the risk that third-party companies will not fully understand the nature and needs of their clients and the fact that such companies have their own bottom lines to meet.

In the past several years, many Fortune 100 companies have begun to move recruiting functions back in-house. One of the primary reasons for this shift is the expanding role of social media and the Internet in recruiting, allowing hiring companies to more easily reach and manage potential recruits. At most, they may hire consulting companies with expertise in developing an online presence and brand. Unlike in the Air Force, "talent acquisition" in industry is an explicit, specialized function of human resources, with people who train and develop skill sets specifically targeted at recruiting new people. In most major companies, it would be inconceivable to pull an engineer, programmer, or line manager from his or her primary duties to serve temporarily in a recruiting role, even in a managerial capacity. The only time non–human resources personnel would be involved in the recruitment process might be to screen potential candidates or perhaps to attend a targeted recruiting campaign that is somehow directly relevant to their area of expertise, such as sending alumni to job fairs at their former universities or anthropologists to an anthropological conference with a recruiting component. Professional recruiters, especially those who are in-house, may not have the operational experience or technical expertise to provide details about specific jobs, but they bring a strong and consistent level of knowledge about how the process of recruiting can work most effectively (Werber, 2015).

The Air Force, and the military more generally, is not an exact parallel for recruiting in industry, as it is important to have a person in uniform available to talk to potential recruits. However, additional office personnel and even managers could certainly be civilians, especially if they are hired or trained as professional recruiters. If it remains important to have an officer in place, the recruiting service might benefit from a team-recruiting approach that would begin by developing recruiting as a core human resources function that could specialize in the requisite skills and techniques—especially those provided by the new social networking environment—rather than relying on the luck of the IR draw. For officers who want to volunteer for these positions, it could even be developed as a dual-track option.

Recruiting in the Other Services

The recruiting process in the other services is largely akin to that in the Air Force. Rather than relying primarily on human resources officers to staff these positions, the services usually treat recruiting as an alternative duty that is spread across a variety of career fields. However, in the past ten years, the Army has piloted a number of programs to incorporate civilians and contractors into its recruiting efforts. One of the largest was a seven-year pilot program that ran from 2001 to 2007, during which numerous recruiting missions were contracted out to ten civilian firms. Recruiters were paid by numbers of recruits, received only three weeks of training rather than the traditional seven weeks, used roughly 20 percent fewer staff than the military units, and relied heavily on veterans as staff (Merle, 2006). While the civilian-run detachments were generally considered less effective, at least half performed within the normal range for all-military control units. In the final analysis, the approach was judged to be a viable option (especially when accounting for broader economic circumstances at the time). Leaders within the Army's recruiting command suggested that federal civilian employees might be a better alternative (Johnson, 2009, pp. 16–17).

Civilian recruiting assistance programs continued in the Army after that point, especially for National Guard and reserve recruiters, with various mixes of military and civilian contractors. In 2012, however, several of these programs were investigated for fraud, which drew wide media attention, causing them to be canceled (O'Harrow, 2012). However, the Army's recruiting command website currently indicates that civilians are indeed incorporated into recruiting stations, suggesting that the Army is still using nonmilitary personnel in a variety of capacities to meet its recruiting needs (U.S. Army Recruiting Command, undated).

Another alternative would be to consider implementing a JROTC-style program for recruiting. As mentioned previously, the Air Force JROTC program hires retired officers and enlisted personnel with certain final rank status and educational qualifications to serve as instructors. These personnel serve in a uniformed capacity and can share their knowledge and experiences with potential accessions, and they are already local to an area, which both increases community ties and decreases the need to relocate or continually train new people. This model could be used to supplement the recruiter positions at detachments and reduce some of the pressure to fill them from the active-duty force.

Recommendations

Alternatives to the current system could reduce the number of active-duty officers required to fill recruiter positions while still ensuring that corporate recruiting targets are met. The reduction in demand for these IR positions may improve overall manning for AFRS and reduce some of the effect on career fields and individuals' career paths. To this end, we offer the following recommendations:

- Incorporate guard, reserve, or retired officers into recruiting detachments, either by providing work hours, combining detachments, or setting up a JROTC-type model.
- Adopt a team-recruiting approach.
- Develop a specialized or dual-track recruiting function within human resources.

Operations C2 and Management: Operations Management (86M0) and C2 (86P0)

Operations C2 and management positions focus primarily on planning, organizing, and controlling operations at command posts, operations centers, and control centers. As of FY 2014, there were 142 authorized positions, but they were internal fills. In other words, they were filled, sometimes as an additional duty, from the population of officers who were already assigned to a given organization or location. Operations C2 and management positions had only a 55-percent manning rate, with 4.2 percent of those fills coming from the rated community. The number of positions has plummeted since FY 2001 (Figure 4.10); the manning rate has increased somewhat since the FY 2007 low of 44 percent. Since only four of these positions are double-billeted and none has been consistently filled by the same career field, solutions involving these avenues are not available. There are, however, a high number of persistent vacancies: Forty-one, or nearly 30 percent, of the positions still on the books in FY 2014 had not been filled for several years. The Air Force should evaluate these positions to make sure they are still valid, particularly given the steep drop in the number of required positions over the past 15 years.

Figure 4.10. Operations C2 and Management: Authorized Positions, Assigned Officers, and Manning, by Fiscal Year

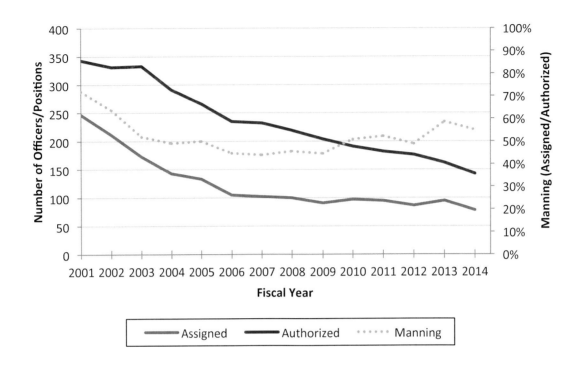

Inspections (87XX)

Inspections positions cover a range of duties and are largely filled internally by the unit, though when a critical inspection position cannot be filled, it is increasingly being sent to AFPC to enter the draft pool. In FY 2014, 107 inspections positions were authorized, with a 55-percent manning rate. The number of these positions spiked in FY 2013, with 40 new positions added in a single year, whereas prior to that, they had been fairly constant (Figure 4.11).[5] Interestingly, 24.3 percent of inspection positions were filled by rated officers—the second highest of all the IR categories—though this level is not an indication that these are particularly desirable positions, rather that rated personnel are available at a given base or are sometimes doing double duty. To match the rapid increase in positions, there was also an increase in people assigned to these positions between FY 2013 and FY 2014, but not enough to offset the increase in positions.

There are ten positions that have been persistently vacant and none that have been continuously filled by the same career field. Even so, because these positions are filled primarily by host units rather than through the IR draft process, reducing their numbers will not have a

---

[5] The inspections IR category is made up of three special-duty identifiers: wing inspector general (87G0); director, wing inspections (87I0); and director, complaints resolution (87Q0). The 87I0 and 87Q0 special-duty identifiers were introduced in 2013, and authorizations were additive to the existing 87G0 identifier with no corresponding IR offset that we were able to identify.

significant effect on the IR process or nonrated career fields. However, validating the new positions from FYs 2013–2014 and eliminating any that are not necessary may reduce the secondary impact of empty positions being sent to AFPC to be filled as part of the draft.

Figure 4.11. Inspections: Authorized Positions, Assigned Officers, and Manning, by Fiscal Year

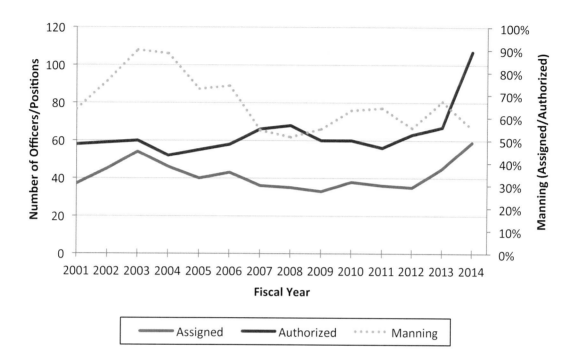

Senior Leader Support: Aide-de-Camp (88A0) and Executive Officer (97E0)

The senior leader support category is composed of aide-de-camp and executive officer positions and involves a variety of duties associated with assisting senior Air Force leaders. Most of these positions are filled internally, though executive officer (97E) positions above the wing level are filled using the IR process. In FY 2014, 313 senior leader support positions were authorized, with 319 officers assigned to those positions (102-percent manning), while 81.2 percent of those positions were filled, of which 20.1 percent were filled with rated officers.

It is interesting to note that despite reductions in personnel and, particularly, headquarters personnel, both the number of senior leader positions and the number of officers assigned has increased substantially over the past decade (Figure 4.12). Though there has been a slight drop in authorizations since the high in FY 2010, there were still 82 more positions and 127 more officers in FY 2014 than in FY 2001. Manning increased in the same time frame, from 83 percent to 102 percent. Much of the aggregate overmanning is due to the number of O-3s and O-4s assigned to executive officer (97E0) positions, as shown in Figure 4.13. Many nonrated line career fields managers have indicated that O-4 positions are the most difficult to fill, so the increase in majors serving in senior leader support roles may exacerbate that situation.

45

Figure 4.12. Senior Leader Support: Authorized Positions, Assigned Officers, and Manning, by Fiscal Year

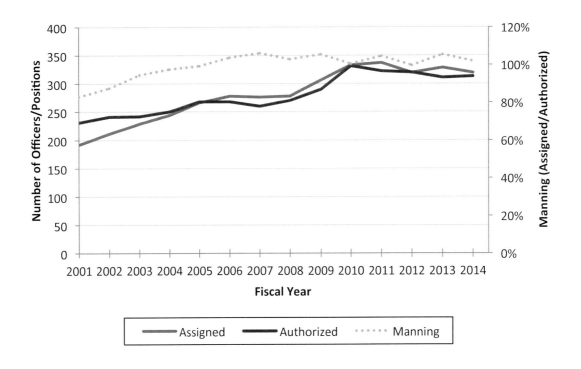

Figure 4.13. Executive Officer (97E0) Authorized Positions, Assigned Officers, and Manning, by Fiscal Year (O-3 and O-4)

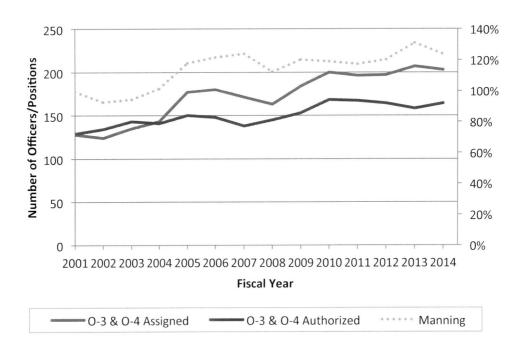

Recommendations

While many senior leader support positions are filled internally and so do not necessarily affect core career fields via the IR draft process, there are two primary ways that the manpower impact imposed by these positions could be reduced:

- **Consider bringing authorizations for senior leader support positions more closely in line with broader Air Force manpower reductions.**
- **Remove persistent vacancies from the authorizations.** While there were only 11 persistent vacancies as of FY 2014, removing these positions could reduce the overall numbers of authorized positions.

Chapter Five. Conclusions and Recommendations

This report examined Air Force IR specialties in detail with the aims of identifying how long-standing undermanning could be improved and determining whether the impact of filling these positions could be lessened for traditional career fields while ensuring that IR-using organizations are staffed with the qualified personnel they need. There are many strategies that the Air Force could pursue to achieve these goals. Some are very tactical in nature. They could be considered normal housekeeping tasks that should be carried out on a regular, periodic basis, such as eliminating positions that are persistently vacant and those that are no longer valid requirements. But other approaches are far more pathbreaking, such as converting some categories of IRs into their own career field or dramatically changing the management of IRs by appointing an individual to serve as a career field manager.

What this diversity of options illustrates is that there is no silver-bullet solution to lessening the impact of IRs. These requirements will persist and are necessary. While there are many opportunities to improve the process, there is no single, one-size-fits-all action that will solve every related problem, especially in the face of Air Force–wide manning challenges. Mitigation and alleviation are perhaps the best that can be hoped for in the short term. To be sure, appointing a career field manager for this disparate set of specialties would bring more order and oversight than exists today. It would provide a focal point whereby requirements and entitlement rates can be regularly reviewed and revalidated. It would give someone responsibility for considering the career effects of serving in these positions and take steps to reduce the stigma that surrounds these assignments. But even that individual and his or her staff will have to take a very deliberate look at each IR category to identify the best courses of action to improve outcomes.

That said, looking across the many recommendations, options, and alternatives presented in this report, several themes stand out:

1. **Get authorizations in order**. A fundamental contribution to undermanning in IRs is undermanning throughout the Air Force. Manning challenges result from how various planning elements—IRs among them—are incorporated into sustainment and accession planning, as well as the general mismatch between authorizations and authorized end strength (which is closely tied to, among other things, the underfunded STP account). Sustainment planning for future IR authorizations based on historical manning rates (which are lower than entitlement) will only exacerbate undermanning in the future. But there are also opportunities to reconcile IR authorizations in IR-using organizations by examining instances of double-billeting, persistent vacancies, and IR positions consistently filled from the same specialties—all cases in which authorizations need to be reviewed and revalidated or perhaps assigned to a core AFSC.

2. **Expand the pool of individuals eligible to fill IR positions**. Many IR positions have strict qualification requirements and need to be filled by active-duty officers to best accomplish the mission. But some categories of positions—instructors and recruiters being two promising examples—may not require active-duty officers in every IR position. The Air Force should examine opportunities to diversify the workforce and consider cases in which guard, reserve, retired military, or civilian personnel may be able to support the mission with equal effectiveness. Doing so will reduce the number of IR positions that must be filled by active-duty officers pulled from traditional career fields.

3. **Tailor approaches for different categories of IRs**. This report offered a rich array of options for lessening the impact of IRs. Some options, such as reconciling authorizations, apply to all categories of IRs and should be an ongoing process. Others, such as creating a distinct career field for particular categories of IRs, apply only to a handful. Again, there is no one-size-fits-all solution. The Air Force will have to examine each IR category carefully, mindful of the unique attributes of each, and tailor solutions appropriately.

4. **Centralized management**. At this point, there is no single individual in the Air Force who is best positioned to evaluate IR categories, perform regular review and revalidation of requirements and entitlement rates, and develop tailored approaches to more efficiently meet IR requirements. A career field manager–equivalent could be provided with the authority to take on these tasks and improve accountability among both IR-using organizations and core career fields. IR positions are necessary and important to the Air Force mission, and a manager of these positions could help ensure that they are filled with the most qualified personnel to meet mission requirements.

Appendix. Manning Levels for Core Career Fields

Table A.1 shows manning levels for nonrated line career fields as of the end of FY 2015. In this table, manning is calculated in two ways. First, it is shown notionally, assuming that officers serve only in their core AFSC. This is not strictly true, but since officer contributions to AFSCs outside of their career fields can vary widely, these numbers indicate the ability of a career field to fill its own positions, given that officers may not be available because they are in training, moving to new assignments (or the other categories of STP), or assigned to IR positions. Second, manning is calculated taking into account officers serving in IR positions from other core AFSCs.

In some cases, the by-grade manning within an AFSC can reveal low manning percentages despite a relatively healthy aggregate manning percentage for the career field as a whole. We categorize manning in Table A.1 as "healthy" for percentages at or above 90 percent, "less than healthy" for percentages between 90 and 75 percent, and "concerning" below 75 percent.

Table A.1. Core AFSC Manning, O-1 Through O-5, End of FY 2015

Legend:	
Manning greater than or equal to 90 percent	●
Manning less than 90, greater than or equal to 75 percent	△
Manning less than 75 percent	◆

Core AFSC	Grade	Authorizations	Inventory	STP	IR Duty	Best Manning without Inter-AFSC lending	Assigned to Core AFSC	Assigned from Other Core AFSCs	Manning with Inter-AFSC Lending
Airfield Operations 13M	O1-O2	57	66	2	0	● 112%	64	8	● 126%
	O3	82	95	1	3	● 111%	90	5	● 116%
	O4-O5	112	109	11	26	◆ 64%	72	3	◆ 67%
	TOTAL	251	270	14	29	● 90%	226	16	● 96%
Missile 13N	O1-O2	463	417	8	1	△ 88%	411	66	● 103%
	O3	315	385	13	19	● 112%	338	45	● 122%
	O4-O5	299	354	27	89	△ 80%	195	9	◆ 68%
	TOTAL	1077	1156	48	109	● 93%	944	120	● 99%
Space 13S	O1-O2	235	424	20	1	● 171%	394	62	● 194%
	O3	603	488	12	47	◆ 71%	395	28	◆ 70%
	O4-O5	630	658	37	147	△ 75%	459	62	△ 83%
	TOTAL	1468	1570	69	195	△ 89%	1248	152	● 95%
Intelligence 14N	O1-O2	402	738	25	2	● 177%	717	69	● 196%
	O3	1284	1126	40	64	△ 80%	1039	45	△ 84%
	O4-O5	1124	967	79	134	◆ 67%	742	3	◆ 66%
	TOTAL	2810	2831	144	200	△ 89%	2498	117	● 93%
Weather 15W	O1-O2	131	124	14	0	△ 84%	112	0	△ 85%
	O3	169	175	12	10	● 91%	156	0	● 92%
	O4-O5	161	194	18	35	△ 88%	136	0	△ 84%
	TOTAL	461	493	44	45	△ 88%	404	0	△ 88%
Cyber 17D/17S	O1-O2	234	501	29	3	● 200%	521	48	● 243%
	O3	965	883	39	64	△ 81%	782	9	△ 82%
	O4-O5	1169	945	78	142	◆ 62%	722	15	◆ 63%
	TOTAL	2368	2329	146	209	△ 83%	2025	72	△ 89%
Aircraft Maintenance 21A	O1-O2	136	320	10	4	● 225%	306	29	● 246%
	O3	492	424	14	37	△ 76%	357	43	△ 81%
	O4-O5	511	503	36	57	△ 80%	329	20	◆ 68%
	TOTAL	1139	1247	60	98	● 96%	992	92	● 95%
Munitions & Missile Maint 21M	O1-O2	37	73	1	0	● 195%	67	2	● 186%
	O3	119	111	7	6	△ 82%	90	8	△ 82%
	O4-O5	130	122	11	8	△ 79%	81	7	◆ 68%
	TOTAL	286	306	19	14	● 95%	238	17	△ 89%
Logistics Readiness 21R	O1-O2	126	354	12	3	● 269%	336	15	● 279%
	O3	400	462	28	47	● 97%	395	2	● 99%
	O4-O5	630	479	33	63	◆ 61%	386	18	◆ 64%
	TOTAL	1156	1295	73	113	● 96%	1117	35	● 100%
Security Forces 31P	O1-O2	148	141	4	0	● 93%	135	1	● 92%
	O3	160	193	10	12	● 107%	171	0	● 107%
	O4-O5	243	266	32	40	△ 80%	193	1	△ 80%
	TOTAL	551	600	46	52	● 91%	499	2	● 91%
Civil Engineer 32E	O1-O2	115	294	38	2	● 221%	251	0	● 218%
	O3	491	374	46	17	◆ 63%	315	1	◆ 64%
	O4-O5	398	407	37	57	△ 79%	313	0	△ 79%
	TOTAL	1004	1075	121	76	△ 87%	879	1	△ 88%

Table A.1. Core AFSC Manning, O-1 Through O-5, End of FY 2015 (Continued)

Legend: Manning greater than or equal to 90 percent	○
Manning less than 90, greater than or equal to 75 percent	△
Manning less than 75 percent	◆

Core AFSC	Grade	Authorizations	Inventory	STP	IR Duty	Best Manning without Inter-AFSC lending	Assigned to Core AFSC	Assigned from Other Core AFSCs	Manning with Inter-AFSC Lending
Public Affairs 35P	O1-O2	27	74	3	1	○ 259%	70	0	○ 259%
	O3	88	101	9	2	○ 102%	93	0	○ 106%
	O4-O5	129	89	4	11	◆ 57%	73	0	◆ 57%
	TOTAL	244	264	16	14	○ 96%	236	0	○ 97%
Personnel 38P	O1-O2	141	343	10	8	○ 230%	327	5	○ 235%
	O3	392	459	16	36	○ 104%	410	3	○ 105%
	O4-O5	506	500	32	74	△ 78%	397	25	△ 83%
	TOTAL	1039	1302	58	118	○ 108%	1134	33	○ 112%
Scientific Analyst 61A	O1-O2	45	107	25	3	○ 176%	75	3	○ 173%
	O3	173	158	32	12	◆ 66%	103	3	◆ 61%
	O4-O5	191	193	21	30	◆ 74%	125	7	◆ 69%
	TOTAL	409	458	78	45	△ 82%	303	13	△ 77%
Behavioral Scientist 61B	O1-O2	14	27	2	1	○ 171%	21	0	○ 150%
	O3	29	42	6	5	○ 107%	29	0	○ 100%
	O4-O5	33	31	3	8	◆ 61%	19	2	◆ 64%
	TOTAL	76	100	11	14	○ 99%	69	2	○ 93%
Chemist 61C	O1-O2	7	21	6	0	○ 214%	13	2	○ 214%
	O3	28	25	9	2	◆ 50%	14	4	◆ 64%
	O4-O5	17	34	4	9	○ 124%	16	1	○ 100%
	TOTAL	52	80	19	11	○ 96%	43	7	○ 96%
Physicist 61D	O1-O2	35	60	14	0	○ 131%	42	1	○ 123%
	O3	81	82	22	8	◆ 64%	49	2	◆ 63%
	O4-O5	85	95	9	9	○ 91%	58	10	△ 80%
	TOTAL	201	237	45	17	△ 87%	149	13	△ 81%
Engineer 62E	O1-O2	582	845	103	5	○ 127%	718	9	○ 125%
	O3	1185	1286	157	90	△ 88%	913	15	△ 78%
	O4-O5	807	1098	105	113	○ 109%	522	26	◆ 68%
	TOTAL	2574	3229	365	208	○ 103%	2153	50	△ 86%
Program Management 63A	O1-O2	260	465	13	9	○ 170%	288	14	○ 116%
	O3	761	635	32	94	◆ 67%	462	118	△ 76%
	O4-O5	1210	857	41	146	◆ 55%	570	352	△ 76%
	TOTAL	2231	1957	86	249	◆ 73%	1320	484	△ 81%
Contracting 64P	O1-O2	108	215	5	8	○ 187%	202	13	○ 199%
	O3	277	275	21	14	△ 87%	235	4	△ 86%
	O4-O5	312	224	12	14	◆ 63%	197	1	◆ 63%
	TOTAL	697	714	38	36	○ 92%	634	18	○ 94%
Financial Management 65F	O1-O2	55	172	18	2	○ 276%	131	0	○ 238%
	O3	165	191	13	25	○ 93%	129	1	△ 79%
	O4-O5	210	228	16	29	△ 87%	176	13	○ 90%
	TOTAL	430	591	47	56	○ 113%	436	14	○ 105%
Special Investigations 71S	O1-O2	72	92	6	0	○ 119%	84	2	○ 119%
	O3	121	124	12	8	△ 86%	105	1	△ 88%
	O4-O5	101	117	9	21	△ 86%	87	0	△ 86%
	TOTAL	294	333	27	29	○ 94%	276	3	○ 95%

References

Air Force Instruction 16-109, *International Affairs Specialist (IAS) Program*, September 3, 2010.

Air Force Instruction 36-2640, *Executing Total Force Development*, December 16, 2008, certified current as of December 29, 2011.

Air Force Instruction 38-204, *Programming USAF Manpower*, April 21, 2015.

Air Force Personnel Center, *Air Force Officer Classification Directory (AFOCD): The Official Guide to the Air Force Officer Classification Codes*, April 30, 2014.

Alrich, Amy A., Joseph Adams, and Claudio C. Biltoc, *The Strategic Value of Foreign Area Officers*, Alexandria, Va.: Institute for Defense Analyses, August 2013.

Biro, Meghan M., "Top 5 Reasons HR Is on the Move," *Forbes*, December 1, 2013. As of July 16, 2016:
http://www.forbes.com/sites/meghanbiro/2013/12/01/top-5-reasons-hr-is-on-the-move

Dong, Yaomin, Jacqueline El-Sayed, and Mohamed El-Sayed, "A Methodology for Team Teaching with Field Experts," *International Journal of Process Education*, Vol. 3, No. 1, June 2011, pp. 43–49.

Dunnette, Marvin D., and Leaetta M. Hough, eds., *The Handbook of Industrial and Organizational Psychology*, Vol. 2, 2nd ed., Boston, Mass.: Nicholas Brealey Publishing, 1995.

Goldman, Charles A., Bruce R. Orvis, Michael G. Mattock, and Dorothy Smith, *Staffing Army ROTC at Colleges and Universities: Alternatives for Reducing the Use of Active-Duty Soldiers*, Santa Monica, Calif.: RAND Corporation, MR-992-A, 1999. As of July 16, 2016: http://www.rand.org/pubs/monograph_reports/MR992.html

Headquarters U.S. Air Force, "Non-Rated Officer Prioritization Plan," briefing, 2001.

Johnson, Fred, *Assessing Cultural Change in the United States Army Recruiting Command*, Carlisle Barracks, Pa.: U.S. Army War College, 2009.

Keller, Kirsten M., Nelson Lim, Lisa Harrington, Kevin O'Neill, and Abigail Haddad, *The Mix of Military and Civilian Faculty at the United States Air Force Academy: Finding a Sustainable Balance for Enduring Success*, Santa Monica, Calif.: RAND Corporation, MG-1237-AF, 2013. As of July 16, 2016: http://www.rand.org/pubs/monographs/MG1237.html

Merle, Renae, "Army Tries Private Pitch for Recruits," *Washington Post*, September 6, 2006. As of July 16, 2016:
http://www.washingtonpost.com/wp-dyn/content/article/2006/09/05/AR2006090501508.html

O'Harrow, Robert, Jr., "Fraud Investigation Targets Recruiting Program for Army National Guard, Reserves," *Washington Post*, March 13, 2012.

Perez, Gustavo, *Measuring the Perceived Transfer of Learning and Training for a Customer Service Training Program Delivered by Line Managers to Call Center Employees in a Fortune 200 Financial Services Company*, dissertation, Denton, Tex.: University of North Texas, 2006. As of July 16, 2016:
http://digital.library.unt.edu/ark:/67531/metadc5401/m2/1/high_res_d/dissertation.pdf

Rabb, Robert, "Team Teaching," West Point, N.Y.: United States Military Academy, Center for Teaching Excellence, 2009. As of July 16, 2016:
http://www.usma.edu/cfe/literature/rabb_09.pdf

Robbert, Albert A., James H. Bigelow, John E. Boon, Jr., Lisa M. Harrington, Michael McGee, S. Craig Moore, Daniel M. Norton, and William W. Taylor, *Suitability of Missions for the Air Force Reserve Components,* Santa Monica, Calif.: RAND Corporation, RR-429-AF, 2014. As of July 16, 2016:
http://www.rand.org/pubs/research_reports/RR429.html

Rothenberg, Alexander D., Lisa M. Harrington, Paul Emslie, and Tara L. Terry, *Using RAND's Military Career Model to Evaluate the Impact of Institutional Requirements on the Air Force Space Officer Career Field*, Santa Monica, Calif.: RAND Corporation, RR-1302-AF, 2017. As of July 2017:
http://www.rand.org/pubs/research_reports/RR1302.html

Rowland, Janette K., and Jennifer Ann Algie, "A Guest Lecturing Program to Improve Students' Applied Learning," *Proceedings of the Australian and New Zealand Marketing Academy Conference*, Dunedin, New Zealand: Australian and New Zealand Marketing Academy, 2007. As of July 16, 2016:
http://ro.uow.edu.au/cgi/viewcontent.cgi?article=2162&context=commpapers

Thie, Harry J., Roland J. Yardley, Peter Schirmer, Rudolph H. Ehrenberg, and Penelope Speed, *Factors to Consider in Blending Active and Reserve Manpower Within Military Units,* Santa Monica, Calif.: RAND Corporation, MG-527-OSD, 2007. As of July 16, 2016:
http://www.rand.org/pubs/monographs/MG527.html

U.S. Air Force, *Occupational Survey Report: Education and Training Utilization Field, Special Duty Identifier, and Technical Instructors*, AFPT 90-75X-911, December 1991. As of July 16, 2016:
http://www.dtic.mil/dtic/tr/fulltext/u2/a245213.pdf

U.S. Army Recruiting Command, "About Us," web page, undated. As of July 16, 2016:
http://www.usarec.army.mil/aboutus.html

Werber, Laura, senior management scientist, RAND Corporation, telephone communication with the author, July 24, 2015.

Wormuth, Christine E., Michele A. Flournoy, Patrick T. Henry, and Clark A. Murdock, *The Future of the National Guard and Reserves: The Beyond Goldwater-Nichols Phase III Report*, Washington, D.C.: Center for Strategic and International Studies, 2006. As of July 16, 2016:
http://csis.org/files/media/csis/pubs/bgn_ph3_report.pdf